Stately**Gardening**

Stately**Gardening**

the changing role of the gardener

Published by VisitBritain Publishing in association with the Historic Houses Association

VisitBritain Publishing
Thames Tower, Blacks Road, London W6 9EL

First published 2007

© British Tourist Authority (trading as VisitBritain) with Susanna Geoghegan Gift Publishing Consultancy 2007

ISBN 978-0-7095-8402-5
Product code: TNSTGAR

A CIP catalogue record for this book is available from the British Library.

Designed and produced for VisitBritain Publishing by Susanna Geoghegan Gift Publishing Consultancy
Printed in China

Contents

Foreword

Stately Gardening forms part of the 'Then and Now' series which has been published in association with the Historic Houses Association (HHA). As its title suggests, the series looks at the life and work of Britain's historic houses today – attracting, as they do, upwards of 15 million visitors a year, providing employment for more than 10,000 people and contributing an estimated £1.6 billion each year to the rural economy – and compares and contrasts this with times past, when these houses and their estates were largely the exclusive preserve of the owners and their guests.

It is a fascinating and inspiring subject, which has been made all the more illuminating thanks to the very considerable help of a large number of people: owners who have set aside time in busy schedules to give interviews and answer questions, administrators who have co-ordinated research, archivists who have made available much valuable material from past and present, members of staff who have broken off what they were doing to chat freely about their work (which in a number of cases spans several decades at the same property).

We extend our very grateful thanks to them all, in particular the following, who have been closely involved with the series throughout its evolution:

At the HHA itself, Peter Sinclair and Fiona Attenborough.

At Ballindalloch Castle, Mrs Clare Macpherson-Grant Russell Laird of Ballindalloch, her husband Oliver Russell and Fenella Corr.

At Chatsworth, the Duke of Devonshire, Simon Seligman, Charles Noble, Stuart Band, Andrew Peppitt, Diana Naylor and Glyn Motley.

At Eastnor Castle, James Hervey-Bathurst, Simon Foster.

At Fonmon Castle, Sir Brooke Boothby.

At Hartland Abbey, Lady Stucley.

At Loseley Park, Michael More-Molyneux, Major James More-Molyneux, Nichola Cheriton-Sutton and Isabel Sullivan (who looks after the Loseley archives at Surrey History Centre).

At Newby Hall, Richard Compton, Robin Compton and Stuart Gill.

At Painswick Rococo Garden, Paul Moir.

At Powderham Castle, the Earl and Countess of Devon, Lady Katherine Watney, Clare Crawshaw, Felicity Harper, Ginny Bowman and Christine Manning.

At Ripley Castle, Sir Thomas Ingilby and Alison Crawford.

In addition we would like to thank three of the above as authors who have kindly permitted us to quote from their work. They, and their books, are: Sir Thomas Ingilby, *Yorkshire's Great Houses* (Dalesman Publishing 2005); James More-Molyneux, *The Loseley Challenge* (Hodder & Stoughton 1995); Clare Macpherson-Grant Russell, *"I Love Food"* (Heritage House Group Ltd 2006).

Introduction

The gardens of historic houses enjoyed their heyday when labour was plentiful and large-scale imports of exotic fruit and vegetables, and freshly cut flowers, had yet to be developed. Variety and productivity was prodigious: at Renishaw Hall in Derbyshire, the Sitwells' head gardener took pride in being able to supply the kitchen with fresh peas for 200 days a year. Arranging year-round displays of fresh flowers, grown in propagating houses, and often changing the principal displays at least twice a day was also the responsibility of the head gardener or one of his staff. Add to this the immaculate maintenance of pleasure gardens, and the need for over thirty garden staff to work outside, and nearly twenty engaged in glass houses can be readily understood.

Renishaw Hall, Derbyshire.

These days gardens and parks of historic houses are open to growing numbers of admiring visitors, although their function and staffing levels have altered significantly. The requirement to grow all the garden supplies for large households has been replaced by the work of small dedicated teams, employing modern technology, to sustain historic gardens, and in some cases rediscover and restore others to their former glory.

The contrast between stately gardening then and now is a fascinating study of adapting and re-focusing traditional skills and designs, while maintaining an aesthetic and horticultural continuity that spans the centuries.

Household Fare

British gardens have been productive as well as ornamental since the Middle Ages. A visit made by William Rufus to the Benedictine Abbey at Romsey in Hampshire, some thirty years after the Norman Conquest led by his father King William I, recorded that the monks kept a garden of roses and herbs. The roses were prized for their fragrance and nourishing qualities, in addition to their symbolic association with the Virgin Mary. The herbs, on the other hand, were put to the practical use of flavouring cooking and preparing medicines.

Over the centuries functional kitchen gardens were separated from elaborate pleasure grounds and intricate parterres. They continued to serve the needs of the household, achieving remarkable levels of productivity and variety, but they did this discreetly, away from the admiring gaze of visitors that was directed at magnificently sculpted vistas and perfectly manicured flower gardens.

Historic houses evolved over the centuries to be largely self-sufficient for food. At Chatsworth, for example, the kitchen garden has been located in three different places since the creation of the first Duke's formal garden at the end of the seventeenth century. It ended up half a mile from the house covering an area of seven acres.

For those with an eye to see, however, kitchen gardens could still offer aesthetic as well as culinary pleasure. William Cobbett, the Regency writer and champion of the poor, commented in 1829 on the delights and rewards of the kitchen garden, writing: 'If well managed, nothing is more beautiful than the kitchen garden: the earliest

blossoms come there: we shall in vain seek for flowering shrubs in March, and early in April, to equal the peaches, nectarines, apricots, and plums; late in April, we shall find nothing to equal the pear and cherry; and, in May, the dwarf, or espalier, apple-trees, are just so many immense garlands of carnations. The walks are unshaded: they are not greasy or covered with moss, in the spring of the year, like those in the shrubberies; to watch the progress of crops is by no means unentertaining to any rational creature; and the kitchen-garden gives you all this long before the ornamental part of the garden affords you anything worth looking at.'

The great age of the kitchen garden reached its zenith in the reign of Queen Victoria and the creation of new kitchen gardens at Frogmore, on the royal estate at Windsor, in 1841 marked a high-water mark. The Act of Parliament that brought these into being rationalised the system that for centuries had supplied the royal household with fruit and vegetables from all the royal gardens within reach. As a result the kitchen garden at Kensington Palace was sold; the one at

Kew was annexed to the botanic gardens; the one at Hampton Court let, while those at Buckingham Palace, Cranbourne Lodge and Cumberland Lodge were put to other uses. From then on the responsibility of provisioning the royal household fell on the newly-constructed kitchen gardens at Frogmore.

This was no small undertaking. A budget of £50,000 was set aside for the project and in the first phases thirty-one acres were brought into cultivation under the supervision of Queen Victoria's head gardener, Thomas Ingram, who played an important part in the 1850s in championing the English Cox apple, which had first been cultivated in the mid-1820s. When the initial acreage proved to be inadequate, a further twenty acres were added and this was augmented in the 1880s by the addition of a four-acre orchard, giving a total extent of fifty-five acres. Although these gardens continue to supply the royal household, they saw their heyday in the closing years of Queen Victoria's reign, as one account written in 1897 shows.

'The finest sight at Frogmore is undoubtedly the conservatories and glass-houses,' it states. 'They are practically without number, as additions are frequently made, and they form a veritable township. The loftiest among them is the Palm House, a really fine structure containing a most valuable collection of palms, ferns, and foliage plants. Next in size is the Conservatory, where are grown every year thousands of splendid camellias, gardenias, and azalea blooms. The camellias in particular are enormous plants.

'The Queen's favourite houses are those devoted to the more delicate kind of roses. These she is very fond of visiting. An interminable quantity of glass is also given up to the cultivation of flowers and foliage of every kind. It is noticeable that Her Majesty has never yielded to the fashionable craze for orchids, and only a small house is given up to the cultivation of a few ordinary kinds at Frogmore. Two houses are, however, filled with the peculiar "carnivorous" plants, which are as uncanny as they are curious, and which emit a most disagreeable odour.

'*The* sight in these most wonderful Royal Gardens is the Pineries. There are eight pits of a total length of four hundred feet. On a hot morning when the pits are opened and each ripening pine sits like a crowned queen on her splendid throne of huge sword-edged grey-green leaves, the sight is most imposing, while the perfume can be scented half-way across the gardens. Pines for the Queen's table are grown of about eight pounds' weight, and are served to her all year round.

'Her Majesty has a fancy only to eat strawberries grown on the Frogmore estate, and wherever she may be, at home or abroad, strawberries are sent to her every day.

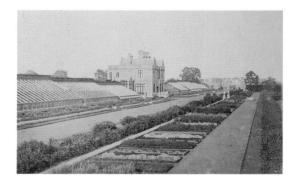

Queen Victoria's gardener and the gardens at Frogmore in the 1870s.

'There being over two miles of wall at Frogmore it is easily understood that the quantity of outdoor fruit grown is immense. Two hundred and fifty varieties of pears alone are cultivated, and the same variety of apples. When fruit is grown under glass, as it ripens, each piece is carefully enclosed in a bag of white tissue paper to prevent wasps or flies from touching it.

'And yet this immense garden – which is divided into eight portions, each under a foreman, who is again responsible to Mr Owen Thomas – is scarcely large enough to supply the Royal Household, and very often there are not enough potatoes produced by the twelve acres devoted to their growth to serve the Royal residences all the year round, and others have to be bought.

'Besides the outdoor asparagus beds, which are in length two thousand two hundred and twenty yards, a great deal of this delicious vegetable is grown under glass; there are also five miles of peas. Of the fruit consumed in the Royal Household the return of one year gives a fair idea.

1,673 dozens of dessert apples,

1,500 dozens and 20 pecks of pears

1,250lbs. of cherries

5,150lbs. of grapes (to which the famous old
vines at Cumberland Lodge and Hampton
Court contribute)

520 dozen peaches

239 pineapples

400 melons

2,700 lbs. of strawberries

1,900 lbs. of gooseberries

220 dozen nectarines

besides quantities of plums, cooking fruit, damsons, and other things. Vegetables are, of course, in like proportion, so it is easy to understand that the hundred and thirty men employed are not idle.

'The Queen and all the Royal Family are great consumers of fruit and vegetables, and believe in their wholesome properties. As with the superfluous farm produce, all the garden produce that is not required at the Castles, is given away among certain people on the Royal estate.

Her Majesty is very well informed on the subject of horticulture, and is, when at Windsor, a frequent visitor to her gardens.

'In Mr Thomas' house, there is a charming room kept sacred to the Queen's use. It is at one end of the building and is entered direct from the wide main walk by a large French window which opens on to two shallow stone steps.

'The wall-paper is blue with rings of gold on it. The furniture of oak with cane seats is very simple, a table fills the centre of the room, and a stuffed cockatoo gives a touch of colour. Here, facing a stone-circled fountain and pond, where some goldfish sport and a sweet-smelling Cape waterweed flourishes, Her Majesty will sit and watch her grand-children riding small bicycles up and down the broad path and swimming boats on the pond.

'The vast daily orders of fruit, flowers and vegetables required for the Castle consumption are received by Mr Thomas from the various departments every morning at a small wooden office which rather disfigures the beautiful old covered court just outside the door of the great kitchen. The Clerk of the Kitchen, the *chef*, and the Table Deckers whose business it is to arrange Her Majesty's board, all state to him what they want. Certain other servants are deputed to change the great plants and palms that stand in the Grand Corridor, while an entirely separate order is given for flowers wherewith to decorate Her Majesty's private apartments. Sometimes, by the Queen's special wishes, flowers are sought for among the woods and hedgerows. In the spring particularly, the Queen likes to see wild flowers in her rooms, and for days at a time bluebells and primroses will replace the rare roses and lilies that are grown at the cost of so much toil and money.'

Similar demands, though on a reduced scale, featured at great houses throughout the country. In large households it was the responsibility of the kitchen garden foreman to supervise the growing of an adequate supply and variety of vegetables all year round. This was no small undertaking as one kitchen garden foreman complained to a newly installed head gardener. 'There are so many departments. There's the dining room, the steward's room, the housemaids, the pantry and the servants' hall, besides the kitchens. It's like feeding a factory.'

In spite of his anxiety and that of others in his position, the kitchens they served never went short. Every morning the vegetables ordered by the head cook were taken to the house, in some cases on a special two-wheeled cart. Standards were rigorously observed. Everything delivered had to be in perfect condition. In spring and summer the head cook might expect to receive radishes, carrots and beetroots bunched, washed and tied with raffia. Anything soiled or damaged would be rejected.

Gardening on this scale enabled head gardeners and their staff to diversify; in the early 1930s the gardens of one stately home produced approaching 400 different varieties of vegetable. Owners took particular pride in serving guests out-of-season fruit and vegetables. Early cucumbers, melons and tomatoes would be grown in propagating houses, where the temperature would be maintained at 80ºF (26.6ºC), so that tomato seed planted in mid-

September produced ripe tomatoes just in time for Christmas, along with new carrots, lettuces, radishes and mushrooms.

Maintaining the correct growing conditions for sensitive plants like these through the long months of winter required constant vigilance. In many country houses the young unmarried men among the garden staff took it in turns to work a 'duty week'. This meant that they had to remain on the premises all the time, keeping the greenhouse boilers stoked with fuel and up to temperature, as well as taking care of the watering, ventilation and general well-being of the plants. Working all day Sunday formed part of the 'duty week', which added to its unpopularity.

Head gardeners charged with providing a constant supply of fresh produce for such a large number of people understandably became very protective of it and were not above taking members of the owning family to task if they injudiciously helped themselves to something they shouldn't. 'If I took a peach from a wall while passing through the garden on a summer's day,'

Typical of many late Victorian houses, the conservatory and
glasshouse required constant attention throughout the year.

recalled the lady of one substantial country house, 'Pomfret [her head gardener] knew at once, and in spite of informing me most politely that one was missing, he managed to convey that he knew perfectly well who the culprit was and that he disapproved strongly.'

As a boy Sir Brooke Boothby recalls being very frightened of some of the staff at his family home at Fonmon Castle, in the Vale of Glamorgan in south Wales. However, he readily acknowledges the deep lifelong affection that they had for the Castle and the estate. The head gardener at the time, Mr Dobbs, typified this. After many years in retirement, during which time stewardship of Fonmon passed to Sir Brooke from his parents, Mr Dobbs woke up one morning in his home in the nearby village of Rhoose and sensed that this was to be no ordinary day. Despite his advanced years, he made his way on foot up to the Castle and the gardens he had loved and tended for so many years. There he chose a favourite spot and lay down. When he was found some time later, Mr Dobbs was dead, at peace in the garden that had been his lifetime's work. A small border named after him marks the spot where he passed away and his family, now living in Australia, return to Fonmon every other year to keep his memory alive.

Glasshouses were an essential prerequisite for gardeners in the production of delicate fruits and exotic flowers and at Chatsworth this 'art' was taken to new heights. This photograph shows the Conservative Wall at Chatsworth subsequently glazed by Paxton in 1848.

Many of our historic houses have special collections
of specific plants or bulbs. The Fuchsia Society was
founded by Lady Boothby in 1938 and her home of
Fonmon Castle has always had exquisite displays,
including the 'Lady Boothby' named variety.

Gardening was a particular interest of Sir Brooke's grandmother and in 1938, following a suggestion made to her by Queen Mary, the Fuchsia Society was founded to further the enthusiasm they both had for fuchsias; the 'Lady Boothby' variety records the work of Sir Brooke's grandmother in this regard. Today the society has branches in sixty countries and its Diamond Jubilee was celebrated at Fonmon in 1998. Her grandson keeps the fuchsia connection . 'We haven't got them all,' he says, 'but we are trying to establish a collection of all the varieties that were hardy outdoor fuchsias in 1938. There were about eighty-five of them, so we should eventually have the whole lot.'

The vegetable gardens at Fonmon have been kept much as they were in days gone by and they still provide produce for Sir Brooke's family as well as the smaller dinners of up to twenty people that are regularly held in the Castle. They contributed to a splendid lunch at the Castle on the occasion of the opening of Wales' Millennium Centre which was given for Sir Donald Gordon, who had donated £10,000,000 to the project. It was attended by the Speaker of the Welsh Assembly and the Economics Minister, as well as senior foreign dignitaries, Sir Donald and his guests. The entire ingredients for the menu – for every course (including the wines) – were sourced from Welsh suppliers, with one exception: the pepper. Try as they might, Sir Brooke confesses, they could not find Welsh pepper anywhere in the principality. Had the dinner been held a few years later, though, even that deficit could have been remedied; in the intervening period the National Botanic Garden of Wales at Llanarthne had successfully produced Welsh-grown pepper.

However, the old frame yard at Fonmon Castle has been converted into a scented garden, partly because it was nowhere near the greenhouses. 'You walked across the main vegetable garden to get to the frame yard,' Sir Brooke explains 'which was up the other side. So we decided to take the frames back down into the bottom vegetable garden next to the greenhouses.'

There's a delightful thatched summerhouse in the scented garden now, and with three doors and a wall closing it off from the rest of the garden, it

A recent development at Fonmon as an adjunct to the
Castle's hospitality provision, the thatched summerhouse
is entirely in keeping with the serenity of its surroundings.

makes a perfect spot for small, private functions that can take place while visitors are still able to enjoy the rest of the garden and grounds.

Powderham Castle, the historic family home of the Earl and Countess of Devon, on the estuary of the River Exe a few miles downstream from Exeter, is located close to the sea like Fonmon. Eighteenth-century records show that the kitchen garden at Powderham produced an extensive range of fruit and vegetables that included Indian jasmine, myrtles and oranges. Two hundred years ago the kitchen garden was even more productive with at least thirteen different varieties of apple, ten varieties of pear, half-a-dozen different kinds of plum and five types of cherry. There were also damsons, greengages, peaches, apricots, nectarines and pineapples. Although these were grown principally to serve the needs of the Castle household, there was clearly enough produced for sales to the public to be entered into the Castle accounts.

By the middle of the nineteenth century, however, the original buildings had fallen into disrepair and a range of new hothouses and sheds were built in their place. Around 1860 a conservatory and peach house were constructed and it seems likely that this coincided with the relocation of the kitchen garden to the site of the present-day Walled Garden.

When the present Countess of Devon first came to Powderham the kitchen garden was still growing fruit, vegetables and cut flowers for the house. 'It was lovely,' she recalls, 'but it is enormous, far bigger than a house this size would have ever needed in its heyday.'

When other financial priorities on the estate forced the closure of the kitchen garden, it raised the question of what to do with the large enclosed space. 'It was sitting there,' Lady Devon continues. 'It's a lovely place – marvellously peaceful in there – and it was another area that we thought could be fun for the public ... Because it's a safe, enclosed area we had the idea of the Secret Garden' – a wonderful pets' corner where children can feed, stroke and enjoy all kinds of domestic and farmyard animals. In 2006 the amenities for young visitors in the Walled Garden were extended by the

construction of the Courtenay Fort: a fabulous wooden castle built by a Cornish company that is proving to be hugely popular with younger visitors and Lord and Lady Devon's grandchildren.

The same kind of imaginative leap was required at Ballindalloch Castle in Banffshire, where Mrs Clare Macpherson-Grant Russell and her family enjoy the matchless setting in which her family has lived since 1546. Gardening twenty miles north-east of Aviemore is not for the faint-hearted, though. With long, cold, wet springs and at least one frost recorded as early as 12 August, 'We are challenge,' as the first Lady Laird of Ballindalloch cheerfully admits. 'Just twenty miles north of us people get the benefit of the Gulf Stream, but we garden in severe conditions. Quite frankly I am delighted with anything that grows, and anyone who wants to know what grows in severe conditions should come here.'

Mrs Macpherson-Grant Russell grew up in Ballindalloch from the age of five, so the climate came as no surprise when she and her husband Oliver returned from London in 1978 to take over the running and welfare of the Castle and estate. Perhaps that awareness put the other challenges in the garden into perspective. They found roe deer and rabbits grazing freely. The one-and-a-half-acre walled vegetable garden comprised grassed-over herbaceous borders and a few apple trees. Added to this, the huge greenhouses in which peaches, melons and exotic house plants had once been nurtured (presumably at unimaginable heating costs) had become so dilapidated that they had to be pulled down. Then there was the rock garden designed by Mrs Macpherson-Grant Russell's grandfather just before the Second World War: 'He was a gardener – he didn't look after the house.'

Fortunately for Ballindalloch, his granddaughter, a Constance-Spry-trained florist, is also an avid gardener and, with her husband, an enthusiastic custodian of this much-loved family home. So the rabbits and deer were persuaded to find nourishment elsewhere, the rock garden was steadily cleared and couch grass that filled the beds was dug out by hand. 'There's plenty left,' the Laird confesses, though she can now find comfort and justified satisfaction at the transformation of the former kitchen garden into something more manageable.

Other financial priorities meant that it would be nearly twenty years after the Russells returned to Ballindalloch before funds were available to redesign the walled garden. 1996 marked the 450th anniversary of the Castle and served as a fitting occasion to undertake the work. The garden designer and author, Suki Urquhart, who aptly described the walled garden's location half a mile away as 'a good brisk walk from the house', was invited to come up with a design. The result is simple, but hugely effective. At the centre stands a stone pond, a focal point around which rows of cherry trees have been planted, and through which rambling roses and clematis thread a screen of colour and delicate fragrance.

Sarah More-Molyneux is another trained florist who exchanged life in London, where she ran her own business, to become the lady of a historic house: in her case Loseley Park near Guildford, the glorious Elizabethan house where her husband

Michael's family have lived since the sixteenth century. Sarah arranges all the flowers in the house and, a keen gardener herself, worked with Michael and their head gardener in the radical transformation of the walled garden at Loseley in the early 1990s.

'At the beginning of the 1900s,' says Michael, 'there would have been something like a dozen gardeners looking after two-and-a-half acres of walled gardens, which supplied the house with

At Ballindalloch the decision to convert the walled kitchen gardens was determined by climate and manpower.

At Loseley Park the walled gardens have been redesigned as a series of productive and decorative areas suited to the needs of the twenty-first-century visitor.

vegetables and fruit. We had an asparagus bed and a carnation house – and so forth. Today, we have two full-timers, three part-timers and some volunteers who come in and dead-head roses … In those days of course, it was all grown to provide for the house and now it is largely grown for the great British public.'

This transition was brought about in large measure by Michael's father, Major James More-Molyneux, a man described by his son as 'always thirty years ahead of his time'. This was certainly the case after the Second World War when Major More-Molyneux pioneered the commercial growing of organic vegetables, which had always

29

A century ago the large number of gardeners employed in great houses allowed very labour-intensive displays and features that would be unsustainable today.

interested him, in the Walled Garden at Loseley – a generation before the organic movement began to register in the public consciousness. For forty years Loseley supplied organic produce for the local market, including Cranks when it opened its first vegetarian food shops in Guildford and then in London.

'By 1993,' as Michael explains, 'my wife and I reckoned you had to move to field-scale for organic vegetable growing. We hadn't got a formal garden at Loseley and with all the interest in gardens – the fact that you can enjoy gardens with no knowledge, from just the colour, the scents, the relaxation and the quiet – creating one seemed the right way to proceed.'

It was quite a change round, Michael admits. 'Over the last ten years it has gone from being an organic market garden to having a rose garden, with a thousand old English roses in it; that was planted in 1993. We then went on to plant a herb garden which has got some 200 different varieties of herbs – one of the biggest of its type in England. There's a fruit and flower garden, which has got annuals in it and is full of colour all the year round, a white garden and a [smaller] organic fruit and veg garden.'

Planning for changes on this scale took a couple of years, beginning in 1990. The revised Walled Garden follows a design influenced by the work of Gertrude Jekyll and was devised as a series of 'rooms'. 'Having literally levelled the garden and having got the top soil absolutely even and straight,' Michael recalls, 'it looked as if an army had been through with napalm. We then marked out all the paths and started to plant these little bits of bracken, which were roses bushes. Everyone said "What on earth have they done?" We asked "What on earth have we done?" And then utterly amazingly next year, on my wife's birthday we had a drinks party in the rose garden with the first blooms appearing.

'We have a wonderful gardener, a Yorkshireman who works eight days a week. He joined us just after the rose garden was planted and he's been with us ever since.'

Just as amazing is the fact that the entire project was conceived and drawn up by Michael and

Not an inch of space is wasted in the production of organic fruit and vegetables at Loseley Park, where part of the garden is allocated to the national heritage seed bank that preserves traditional varieties of kitchen garden produce.

Sarah's former nanny, who had taken a garden design course after helping to raise the four More-Molyneux children. 'It was quite a feat,' Michael says admiringly, 'for someone whose first commission it was to achieve what she did.'

Although the revised vegetable garden at Loseley is nothing like the size of its predecessor, it still provides fresh fruit and vegetables for the More-Molyneux family throughout the year. So varieties are chosen, as they are in any productive garden, to come to maturity when the vegetables are most needed. Carrots, for example, are planted depending on whether sweet baby carrots are needed, or ones that will store well over the winter.

Jane Jennifer, who looked after this area of the Walled Garden at Loseley for several years, followed seminal principles that have become established practice among organic gardeners everywhere. So a system of crop rotation has been established to reduce the build-up of soil-borne pests and diseases that target particular families of vegetables, and to enable an appropriate taking and giving of nutrients and conditioners at all levels of the soil.

Many of the vegetables are cultivated in small permanent beds, narrow enough for the centre to be reached from the path. Such a system promotes good soil structure, which might otherwise be damaged by digging in wet conditions, or simply from being repeatedly trodden on. Narrow bed planting also allows for an efficient use of all manures, composts and mulches, and it enables plants to be grown close together, thereby inhibiting weed growth.

Another principle successfully practised at Loseley is companion planting, the system that sees particular herbs and flowers being grown alongside fruit and vegetables. These may encourage aphid-eating predators; they may be at work below ground level, promoting the good health of the fruit and vegetables growing beside them; they may simply be acting as a green manure, nourishing soil that will be brought into cultivation later in the season. 'At Loseley,' writes Jane Jennifer in her guide to the organic vegetable garden there, 'we use those plantings that make sense to us (such as growing open-structured flowers with easily accessible pollen to

33

attract useful, aphid-eating insects) and we try out other companion plantings if we experience a problem that is challenging to us (such as undersowing brassicas with clover, trefoil, lettuce or basil to deter brassica flea beetle). In these latter situations, it is through experience and close observation that we determine whether or not the practice appears useful and is worth trying to replicate.'

Past and present are brought satisfyingly together in the vegetable garden at Loseley, where one area is given over to the growing of old-fashioned varieties of vegetables specifically for seed production. Loseley is one of fourteen Heritage Seed Library Gardens in the country set up under the auspices of Garden Organic, the working name of the Henry Doubleday Research Association (HDRA), which has been at the forefront of promoting and researching organic gardening since 1954. The HSL beds at Loseley were established exactly fifty years later and provide seed of old and unusual vegetables for planting in the garden as well as contributing towards the national seed bank.

The need for such a conservation measure came about as a result of EU regulations forbidding the sale of any vegetable seeds that had not been officially registered in national or EU catalogues. Since the annual cost of registration runs into hundreds of pounds, seeds with only a modest commercial return were not registered and began to disappear. Despite changes in the legislation, some varieties of vegetable are threatened with disappearance, which makes the schemes at Loseley and elsewhere all the more important.

Ripley Castle, near Ripon in North Yorkshire, is another historic house that has given over part of its vegetable garden to HSL production. Sir Thomas Ingilby, whose family have been living at Ripley uninterrupted for almost 700 years, explains, 'We take about thirty seed varieties each year, propagate them and then send the seed back to the HDRA and in that way grow the stock. In the meantime visitors can come and see the varieties actually growing here.

'We reckon that 300 or 400 visitors come every year specifically to see this rare veg collection, because people have their own allotments, their

With both small domestic gardeners and large estates all needing an annual supply of fresh seed, seedmen such as those at Holgate near York used to be found in every major town.

own kitchen gardens and they love comparing our vegetables with the ones they grow at home. And, boy, do they tell us if their veg are better than ours! ...

'I have actually been stopped by a visitor,' he recalls with amusement, 'who recognised me and said "What are you going to do about your whitefly?" Not being a gardener, I'm afraid I was completely stuck for an answer. Shooting them didn't seem like the right suggestion.'

One of the gardeners working at Ripley is a keen allotment gardener and concentrates almost exclusively on growing the vegetables. The HSL

crop is purely for seed propagation, so a large bed, beautifully maintained, in the centre of the kitchen garden serves as a working garden supplying soft fruit, salad ingredients and vegetables to the catering kitchens in the Castle and the nearby Boar's Head Hotel, which is also part of the Ripley estate.

Efficient and productive, this is also immensely satisfying. 'It's very common to see chefs running out here in their check trousers and white jackets, with baskets, to cut things and take them back into the kitchens,' says Sir Thomas. 'You see that most days – and the gardeners and chefs

will get together to decide what they're going to need and what they can use: what recipes they will put on each week to make use of what we're growing here.'

There is a herb garden at Ripley, as there is at Loseley, and as there could well have been at both houses in past centuries supplying culinary and medicinal herbs for the household. During the holidays the Ingilby children help out on the estate

From garden to kitchen is still a short step at Ripley Castle where chefs and gardeners regularly plan the best use of seasonal produce.

and their parents are pleased that the next generation is already developing an interest in the history of the gardens. Sir Thomas's 19-year-old son, Joslan, with his interest in history, is particularly fascinated by the medical and culinary applications of the many plants in the herb garden.

Herb borders line the central path and big vegetable beds in the revived kitchen garden at Chatsworth. The original seven-acre kitchen garden, which fell into decline after the Second World War, was brought back into life in 1994 after three years of intensive work, during which new drains were laid, raised beds were built and cold frames restored. As a result, the house can once again be supplied with vegetables grown here, and lettuces and other salads can be supplied to the Carriage House Restaurant

The kitchen gardens at historic houses such as Powderham, Ripley, Loseley and Chatsworth just serve present-day requirements; it would be profligate to attempt to do otherwise. However, the recently restored Rococo Garden at Painswick in Gloucestershire up on the Cotswold escarpment above the city of Gloucester (described in greater detail later) has reinstated the original kitchen garden as depicted in a painting of it dating from 1748. A century later the geometry of the eighteenth-century kitchen garden had disappeared. By the twentieth century the original design of the garden had vanished completely and most of the six acres of the valley in which it lay had been filled with different sized plots given over to the growing of vegetables and soft fruits. Five full-time gardeners worked in this large kitchen garden until 1955, with no machinery to help them apart from a small motor mower. However, this kind of market gardening was unsustainable and, by the mid-1960s, the owner Lord Dickinson had little option but to close down the garden and plant a wood on the site.

As a result of over twenty years of restoration work, the geometric layout of the original kitchen garden has been recreated, based on evidence from the 1748 painting and archaeological surveys that revealed the positioning of its paths. A network of contemporary apple and pear trees, trained as espaliers, now acts as divisions between the main areas, where eighteenth-century varieties of fruit and vegetables are grown wherever possible. This produce is used in the popular garden restaurant – a timely service that appeals to the growing numbers of visitors who are concerned about 'food miles' and the huge distances over which even common or garden produce is sometimes transported these days.

At Painswick Rococo Garden it could be argued that the kitchen garden had come full circle in 250 years: from production, to disappearance and back to production once again. However, such a

In the process of being restored to its former eighteenth-century design after 'disappearing' for over a century, the kitchen garden at Painswick Rococo Garden has been modelled using a 1748 painting of the garden for reference.

conclusion would overlook the fundamental difference between kitchen gardens 'then and now'. Historically, they existed to supply fresh fruit, vegetables and cut flowers to the great house.

Cloches (mini glasshouses) were often deployed in large numbers to bring on early vegetables, unsuited for growing in greenhouses, to satisfy the demands for out-of-season supply.

Indeed, the ability to serve perfect produce and luxurious fruits from one's own gardens was a source of great pride in many country houses – even if kitchen gardens were kept out of sight and seldom merited the attention of visitors. Today, as we have seen, the produce grown in the kitchen gardens of historic houses supplies the needs of the family, just as any family garden or allotment does. The main focus, however, is in contributing to the catering needs of the lucrative hospitality businesses on which the financial security and development of so many historic houses increasingly depends.

Another crucial factor affecting kitchen gardens in particular (and formal gardens in general) is tailoring the work to suit the numbers employed to do it. Victorian kitchen gardening was enormously labour intensive, as were the formal gardens with crisply clipped, knife-edged box hedges marking out perfectly manicured parterres and yards of industriously weed-free herbaceous borders. Changes in fashion largely dictated the numbers of gardeners employed in a historic house. In the last quarter of the

The gardens at Alton Towers, photographed in 1898 when it was still a private home, illustrate how labour intensive the maintenance of high Victorian gardens had become.

eighteenth century, when the gardens at Chatsworth were uncultivated for the most part, forming part of 'Capability' Brown's landscaped park, the annual wages bill for garden staff was £100 a year. Sixty years later, the gardens designed and overseen by Joseph Paxton – the ones that so enthralled Queen Victoria, as we will discover later – generated annual labour costs of

41

£3,000. Sixty years on, at the beginning of the 1900s, there were eighty people employed in the gardens at Chatsworth.

That marked the watershed, not for Chatsworth alone, but for every great house, indeed for every house where several gardeners traditionally had been employed. In just five years, between 1907 and 1912, the number of under-gardeners almost halved at Chatsworth, falling from fifty-five to twenty-nine. During that same period the annual salary paid to the head gardener rose by forty pounds from £140 to £180; in addition he received, in 1912, a house in the kitchen gardens, 'rent, rate and tax free', two dog carts 'provided and maintained for his use' and unlimited supplies of gas and coal. An interesting sideline on the economic climate of the time is that the estimated rental value of his house remained unchanged between 1907 and 1912, at twenty-seven pounds ten shillings.

Today mechanisation and simplified garden maintenance means that a team of a little over twenty gardeners – divided into three groups to look after the pleasure grounds, vegetable gardens and greenhouses – can keep on top of the work in all 105 acres of the Chatsworth gardens and maintain them to the same high standards with which they have always been treated.

Sir Thomas Ingilby emphasises the kinds of changes that have taken place in his book *Yorkshire's Great Houses*, in which he writes, 'The burgeoning interest in gardens and gardening has radically altered the management philosophy that applies to them. The large formal garden areas that accompanied many stately homes once lost substantial sums of money. They were designed to be maintained by a dozen or more gardeners, but today that would cost in the region of £200,000 a year in salaries, expenses and national insurance, and such cost would be completely uneconomical when set against the likely visitor revenue. The use of labour-saving devices – tractor mowers, strimmers, rotavators and hedge cutters – enabled more work to be carried out by fewer people in less time. Lawns that used to take three men the best part of a week to mow could now be done by one person in less than a day with a tractor mower.'

(Anyone who has ever used an old-fashioned cylinder mower that needs pushing by hand will know how arduous and time-consuming that can be. However, even that marked a huge advance on cutting a lawn using a scythe, a technology that had hardly changed since Roman times.

Admittedly large lawns would have been cut by several men with several scythes, as Sir Thomas Ingilby suggests, and they would have been replaced by a large cylinder mower drawn by a donkey or pony wearing leather boots to prevent it criss-crossing the newly cut sward

The extensive lawns found in the grounds of most historic houses required significant manpower to maintain their pristine appearance. Formerly scythed by hand, the advent of the horse- or donkey-drawn grassmower represented a significant development in lawn maintenance.

with semi-circular hoof prints, but the process was still painfully slow compared with what can be achieved today with even a domestic lawnmower.)

But back to Sir Thomas, who draws the conclusion that, 'The remaining labour could be far more profitably applied at the new plant centre.

'Stately home owners, gardeners and managers watched the growth of garden centres with interest, and realised that they could capitalise on the fashion. They had the space. They had the visitors. They had the room in which to grow large stocks of plants. They had the gardeners and the knowledge of plants. If it transformed the gardens from a loss-making enterprise into one that paid its way, thereby securing jobs, the gardeners were all in favour of it.'

Sir Thomas draws on the example of John Foxton to illustrate his point. For many years he tended the gardens and grounds at Castle Howard. A little over twenty years ago he was asked if he would like to manage the plant centre there, effectively running his own part of the overall estate business, responsible for his own budget and his own team.

A gardener through and through, John Foxton discovered a new talent as a manager and entrepreneur. 'I still get a lot of pleasure from growing good-quality stock,' he said in an interview, 'but nowadays I get as much pleasure from the contact I have with regular customers – many of them local people I have known for decades.'

Centuries of continuity have been maintained by John Foxton and gardeners in historic houses up and down the country; the role they now fulfil may have been adjusted to cater for present-day requirements, but in this too they are simply reflecting a pattern of evolution and change, as old as the houses and estates where they work, that they and their predecessors have followed down the centuries.

Even when animal-drawn mowers were already in general use there were situations where the scythe was still indispensable.

Gardens of Delight

There is nothing new about stately homes welcoming visitors. Many historic houses were opening their doors and their gardens to interested sightseers generations before the need arose to do this as a commercial venture. The guidebook to Chatsworth informs the reader that the house and garden have been 'open for people to see round for most of the time since it was built … In 1775 an inn (now the estate office and club) was built at Edensor for the convenience of sightseers.'

In the middle of the nineteenth century Chatsworth and its garden attracted particular attention during the time that the Sixth Duke of Devonshire was making significant alterations and additions. In February 1844 an entry in *The Mirror of Literature and Amusement* noted, 'The Duke of Devonshire allows all persons whatsoever to see the mansion and grounds every day in the year, Sundays not excepted, from 10 in the morning till 5 in the afternoon. The humblest individual is not only shown the whole, but the Duke has expressly ordered the waterworks to be played for everyone without exception. This is acting in the true spirit of great wealth and enlightened liberality; let us add, also, in the spirit of wisdom.'

Chatsworth is one of a good many historic houses, with roots stretching back to the time of the first Queen Elizabeth, that retain vestiges of their Elizabethan gardens. The elaborate knot gardens and parterres made up of intricate flower beds sharply defined by clipped hedges and gravel paths may have been erased by developments in later centuries, but the spaces they once occupied survive in many gardens as elegant manicured lawns.

The tradition of highly formal and elaborate design stretches back to Elizabethan times and this 1699 engraving of the grounds at Chatsworth typifies this long tradition.

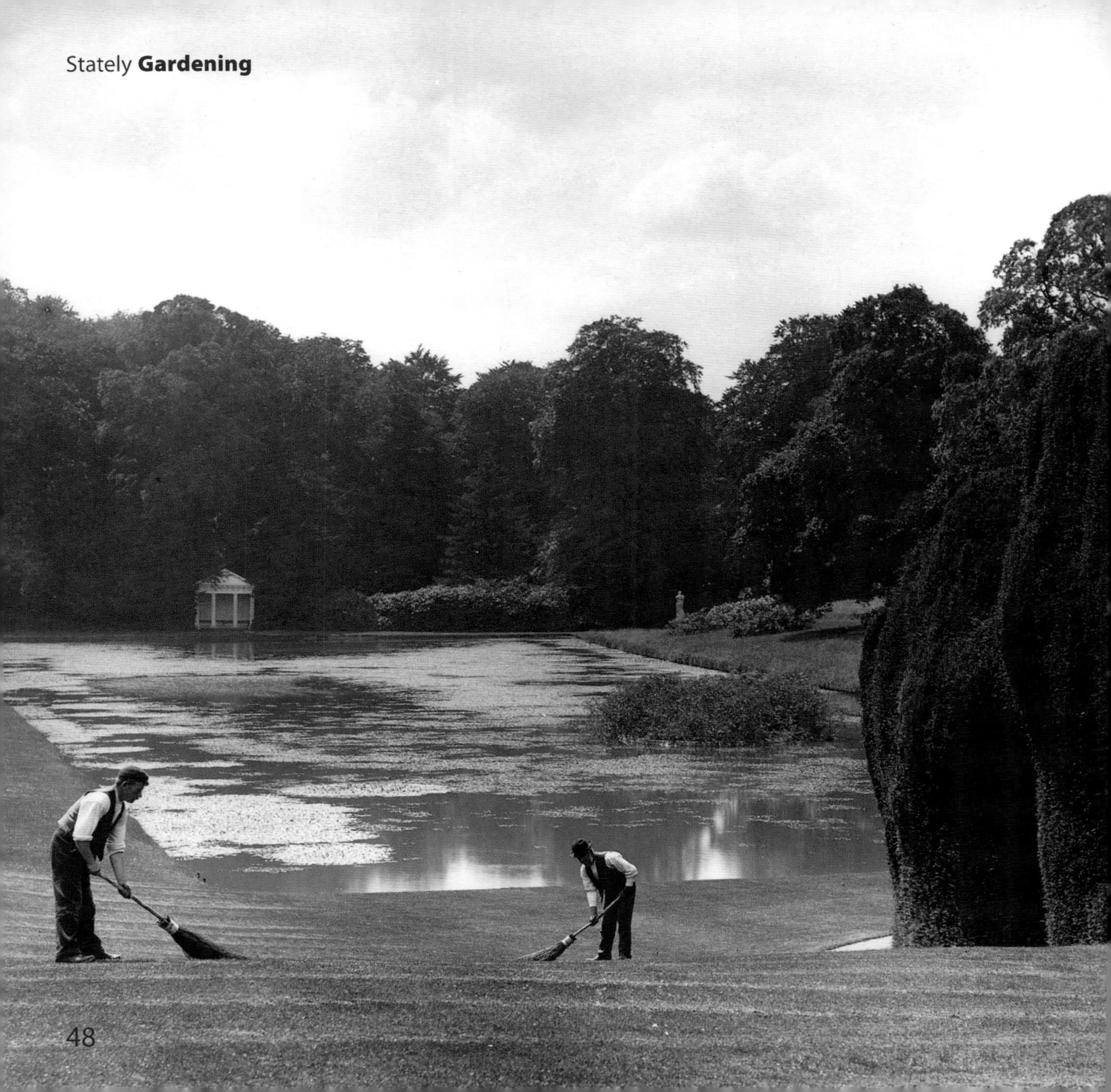

The philosopher and statesman Sir Francis Bacon took a keen interest in the relationship between Man and Nature and, writing four hundred years ago, set down the principles of Renaissance garden design he so admired. 'The garden is best to be square,' he observed, 'encompassed, on all four sides, with a stately arched hedge. The arches to be upon pillars of carpenter's work, of some ten foot high and six foot broad; and the spaces between of the same dimension with the breadth of the arch. Over the arches let there be an entire hedge, of some four foot high. Framed also upon a carpenter's work and upon the upper hedge, over every arch, a little turret, with a belly, enough to receive a cage of birds; and over every space between the arches some other little figure, with broad plates of round coloured glass, gilt, for the sun to play upon. But this hedge I intend to be raised upon a bank, not steep. But gently slope, of some six foot, set all with flowers. Also I understand that this square of the garden should not be the whole breadth of the ground, but to leave, on either side, ground enough for diversity of side alleys; unto which the two covert alleys of the green may deliver you. But there must be no alley with hedges at either end of this great enclosure: nor at the hither end, for letting your prospect upon this fair hedge from the green; not at the further end, for letting your prospect from the hedge, through the arches upon the heath.'

By the middle of the eighteenth century, the discipline and geometric symmetry that characterised Renaissance gardens was giving way to the freer canvas of landscape gardening, which saw the destruction of many formal gardens. Foremost among the professional landscape gardeners engaged to transform English estates was Lancelot Brown, famous now for identifying the 'great capabilities' in the 100 or more landscapes he was commissioned to improve, and for the nickname by which he is widely remembered: 'Capability' Brown.

His work, like that of garden designers in every century, reflected the taste and fashion of his time. By the middle of the eighteenth century a

Large estates provided a blank canvas for the fullest expression of the theories of the eighteenth-century English landscape movement. At Chatsworth the lie of the land was ideal for 'Capability' Brown's vision.

combination of an education in the writings of classical Greek and Latin authors, coupled with a Grand Tour of Continental Europe (and Italy in particular), steeped the heirs of most great English houses in the romantic ideals of Arcadian scenes that dominated European landscape painting and garden design. What they saw on their travels, many sought to replicate at home and they turned to the likes of Brown and Humphry Repton, who succeeded him, to transform their visions into vistas that have come to symbolise the English landscape movement.

In this they were supported by contemporary literature as well as art. The poet Alexander Pope united all three when he made his oft-quoted pronouncement, 'All gardening is landscape painting.' He went further in the poem he addressed to his friend Lord Burlington in 1731, in which he expressed the importance of working in harmony with the natural environment. 'In all, let Nature never be forgot,' the poet urges:

> But treat the Goddess like a modest fair,
> Nor over-dress, nor leave her wholly bare;

A few lines later he puts in words many of the characteristics that landscape designers would soon be incorporating into their improvements: meandering rivers or curving lakes, contoured expanses of cropped turf and clumps of trees all leading the eye to a distant prospect of soft green woodland.

Consult the Genius of the Place in all;
That tells the waters or to rise or fall,
Or helps th' ambitious Hill the heav'n to scale,
Or scoops in circling theatres the Vale,
Calls in the County, catches opening glades,
Joins willing woods, and varies shades from
    shades,
Now breaks or now directs, th' intending Lines;
Paints as you plant, and, as you work, designs

The concept of reading a landscape was one that Brown would have approved of, since he frequently described his work in literary or grammatical terms, 'Now, there I make a comma, and there where a more decided turn is proper, I make a colon; at another part, where an interruption is desirable to break the view – a parenthesis – now a full stop; and then begins another subject.'

Humphry Repton, whose influence on landscape design can still be widely seen, set his own criteria for 'what a garden is, and what it ought to be'. In his opinion, 'It is a piece of ground fenced off from cattle, and appropriated to the use and pleasure of man: it is or ought to be, cultivated and enriched by art, with such products as are not natural to this country, and, consequently, it must be artificial in its treatment, and may, without impropriety, be so in its appearance; yet, there is so much of littleness in art, when compared with nature, that they cannot well be blended; it were, therefore, to be wished, that the exterior of a garden should be made to assimilate with park scenery, or the landscape of nature; the interior may then be laid out with all the variety, contrast, and even whim, that can produce pleasing objects to the eye.'

Artists, writers and aristocrats were not alone in taking an active interest in designing gardens and the houses they were created to complement. Horace Walpole, the eighteenth-century politician and social commentator became an enthusiastic visitor to great houses, though even he was not immune to the tedium and occasional discomfort that guests at house parties of the period sometimes endured in the course of enjoying hospitality indoors and in the gardens. In 1770 Walpole joined a house party at Stowe (where 'Capability' Brown had once served as head gardener) given in honour of George II's second daughter, Princess Amelia, and made the following observations about his visit to this famous house (which is now a public school) and its equally famous garden.

'We breakfasted at half an hour after nine,' Walpole wrote, 'but the Princess did not appear till it was finished; then we walked in the garden, or drove about in cabriolets till it was time to dress; dined at three which, though properly proportioned to the smallness of the company to avoid ostentation; lasted a vast while, as the Princess eats and takes a great deal; then again

Walpole's 'grotto in the Elysian Fields'.

into the garden till past seven, when we came in, drank tea and coffee, and played at pharaoh till ten, when the Princess retired and we went to supper and before twelve to bed. You see there was great sameness and little vivacity in all this. It was a little broken by fishing and going round the park one of the mornings; but in reality the number of buildings and variety of scenes in the garden made each day different from the rest ...

'On Wednesday night a small Vauxhall was acted for us at the grotto in the Elysian Fields, which was illuminated with lamps, as were the thicket and the two little barks on the lake. The idea was really pretty, but as my feelings have lost some of their romantic sensibility, I did not quite enjoy such an entertainment *al fresco* as I should have done twenty years ago. The evening was more than cool and the destined spot anything but dry. There were not half lamps enough and no music but an ancient militia man who played cruelly on a squeaking tabor and pipe. As our procession descended the vast flight of steps into the garden, in which was assembled a crowd of people from Buckingham and neighbouring villages to see the Princess and the show, the moon shining very bright, I could not help laughing, as I surveyed our troop which, instead of tripping lightly to such an Arcadian entertainment, were hobbling down the balustrades wrapped up in cloaks and great-coats for fear of catching cold. The Earl, you know, is bent double, the Countess very lame, I a miserable walker, and the Princess, though as strong as a Brunswick lion, makes no figure in going down fifty stone stairs ... We were none of us young enough for a pastoral. We supped in the grotto, which is as proper to this climate as a sea-coal fire would be in the dog-days [of high summer in late July and early August] at Tivoli ...'

Despite Horace Walpole's misgivings, the objective in every case was to create a garden that would bring pleasure to all who saw it and had the chance to enjoy it. The scale of the work involved may have been awesome, but the results are timeless. It has been calculated that the changes carried out at Chatsworth in accordance with Brown's design involved 25,000 man days of work and a similar number of horse days. When these statistics are spread across the intervening centuries separating the 1760s and today, they amount to two man days and two horse days of labour a week for each of the 240 or so years – a sound investment, one might argue.

The nineteenth century saw a return to the formality of Renaissance gardens, and high Victorian gardens were characterised by intricately sculpted beds filled with brightly coloured bedding plants. These were gardens designed for display and entertainment, for tea on the lawns, leisurely strolls and an escape from the grime and bustle of the city. The pleasure owners took in their country houses was reflected by the thoughts expressed by Sir John Williams when he wrote to Mary Lucy of Charlecote Park in 1844, 'How pleasant to find yourself in easy slippers, running from one flower-bed to another in the fine old Court, little toes relaxed on the turf after the hard flags of London! How delicious to pick a Strawberry, and smell a Rose, and kiss the sweet cheeks of your chicks and turn about in ease and comfort, instead of walking up to a Glass to find out the blacks on your nose, or to shake off the park dust from your beautiful ringlets.'

Exotic species imported from the colonies took root in nineteenth-century English gardens too, as did the passion for colossal conservatories and winter gardens, where opulently heated ferns and tropical plants defied the vagaries of the English climate. Joseph Paxton, who constructed the famous Crystal Palace, built for the Great Exhibition of 1851, served as head gardener at Chatsworth from 1826. Under his guidance the famous Emperor Fountain was created, as were the Pinetum and the Arboretum. These can still be enjoyed today, though Paxton's achievement at Chatsworth most celebrated among his contemporaries, the Great Conservatory, lasted just eighty years before it was demolished in1920.

Begun in 1836, this enormous building, the largest conservatory in the world, took four years to build and was planted out in 1840. Three years later, in December 1843, Queen Victoria and Prince Albert paid a visit to Chatsworth accompanied by a distinguished retinue. The *Illustrated London News* gave fulsome coverage to the event, in which Paxton's Great Conservatory and the gardens in general took centre stage, even in the depths of winter. On the afternoon of the Queen's arrival, the royal party toured the state rooms after which, as the report runs, 'Her Majesty then signified her wish to see the conservatory, a building and collection of plants so grand and so rare as to be deservedly ranked among the minor wonders of England. To this she was conducted by the Duke and attended by the guests.

'The Grand Conservatory … is 300 feet long by 145 feet wide and covers about *an acre of ground*. The elevation of the central covered roof is 67 feet, with a span of about 70 feet, resting upon two rows of elegant iron columns. Round the centre at the base of the dome, is carried a gallery; and directly through the centre is a spacious carriage-drive. From an elevation of four feet from the ground is one mass of glass; each plate being 4 feet long by 6 inches wide: the ascent to the gallery is by steps of rock work, covered with rare plants. By means of tanks, a circulation of hot and cold water is kept up, through tubes occupying six miles in length. The sash-bars [which Paxton cleverly designed to collect external rain water and internal condensation], if laid end to end

would reach forty miles length; and they contain 70,000 square feet of glass. Mr. Paxton, F.L.S., is the sole contriver and architect of this wonderful conservatory. Such is its extent and convenient arrangement, that as many as three or four carriages have been driven in it at one time. Among the vegetable Titans are the *Arbutelon Striatum*, 20 feet high, *Corypha Umbraculifera*, or gigantic palm; the dwarf plantain, a banana, one plant of which bore 300 fruit last year.'

From the conservatory the royal party made their way to the west terrace where Queen Victoria had planted a tree eleven years earlier, when she had visited Chatsworth as a child. On this occasion, Prince Albert planted a tree of his own to grow beside his wife's. As the *Illustrated London News* recorded, 'He selected an oak sapling, and planted it with all due formality' before going on to note, 'As her Majesty appeared at those points of the grounds, of which view could be obtained from without, she was cheered in the most enthusiastic manner by multitudes of people there assembled.'

If the Great Conservatory and gardens appealed to the royal visitors by day, the impact they made at

Predating the Crystal Palace by a decade, Paxton's 1840 Great Conservatory for Chatsworth was the focal point of Queen Victoria's royal visit in 1843. An engineering feat and a mark of prestige for the owners, this was the largest conservatory in the world.

night was truly memorable. 'At six o'clock [in the evening of their second day at Chatsworth] her Majesty, the Prince, the Duke of Wellington, the Duke of Devonshire and other distinguished personages, visited the grand conservatory which was brilliantly lighted with [14,000] lamps, disposed along the ribs, by which the sides of this magnificent structure are divided, in a very tasteful manner. The effect of the scene was comparable to the fairy palace of some eastern tale.

'Her Majesty and Prince Albert entered one of the duke's chariots: the Earl of Jersey and her Majesty's noble host seated themselves in the dicky behind the carriage, and, followed by two pony phaetons, the party passed from the entrance arch into the park, and proceeding up the winding carriage-road leading to the heights, and through the magnificent rockery now in progress of formation, entered the conservatory. The military band on the terrace played the national anthem. At the entrance her Majesty was received by Mr. Paxton, who had the honour of showing to the Queen and her royal consort the matchless collection therein. Her Majesty, before the carriage had reached the east end of the conservatory, alighted, and, accompanied by her suite, then minutely inspected the shrubs and plants, and in allusion to the artificial decoration by lamps remarked that "It was indeed a fairy scene and gave her the highest possible delight." The prince also, upon entering, emphatically exclaimed, "This is most beautiful." …

'During the time that the royal party were dining [in the grand dining-room in the house] the public were admitted (by ticket) to view the conservatory.

'About ten o'clock, commenced a magnificent display of fireworks. The noble cascade was lit up with many coloured fires, and the whole extent of the gardens was a blaze of light. The Queen, Prince Albert, and the rest of the distinguished party enjoyed the magnificent scene from the windows of the south front. The Duke of Wellington, while contemplating the scene, is known to have remarked:—"I have travelled Europe through and through, and witnessed scenes of surpassing grandeur on many occasions, but never before did I see so magnificent a *coup d'oeil* as that now extended before me."'

Sadly the Great Conservatory proved to be unsustainable. Every winter its eight huge boilers consumed 300 tons of coal. During the First World War many of the delicate plants died through shortages of fuel to warm them and gardeners to look after them. When peace was restored in 1918, the Great Conservatory was a sad sight and two years later it was decided to demolish the building.

This expansive and wonderfully ornate conservatory at Enville Hall, Staffordshire, photographed in 1901, was deemed to be a triumphant expression of the local glass and iron industries.

Explosive charges were placed on the main supports; when these were detonated, according to one eyewitness, 'we first heard the explosion and then saw the glass go scintillating up into the air. It was a sad occasion as it was so beautiful.'

All that remained of Paxton's great structure were the sandstone walls of its foundation. However, in 1962 a maze was planted on the site to supply another attraction to the large number of visitors drawn to Chatsworth every year.

Providing facilities that attract large numbers of visitors is now a paramount concern to the owners of historic houses and gardens. No longer is it enough to impress and dazzle one's peers and the occasional royal visitor. Gardens these days have to earn their keep along with every other estate enterprise and settling on the most suitable way of achieving this requires clear thinking and a delicate balancing act.

Newby Hall, near Ripon in North Yorkshire, has another of the most famous gardens in England. Created and cherished by three generations of the Compton family, it stands as a landmark for garden preservation and maintenance in the difficult post-war years, when the gardening in so many historic houses was scaled down and had to take second place to re-jigging estate income and keeping a sound roof on the house itself.

Robin Compton, who inherited Newby from his father in 1977, was a businessman by profession. Fortunately for the gardens he took over, he and his wife are also passionate gardeners. So it was, while his father was still alive and still running the estate, and while Robin was still in business, that he drew up a ten-page master plan, *Newby in the Seventies*, in which he laid down what he thought should happen to his family's home for over 250 years.

And what did he see when he looked into the future?

His son, Richard, who has taken on the stewardship of Newby ably helped by a team of professional 'heritage' managers, answers in one word, 'Children … children … children.'

'Reading it, when father handed over to me six, seven years ago,' Richard says, 'the one thing that

One of many delightful garden vistas at Newby Hall.

he saw, which previous generations hadn't seen, was that children were beginning to dominate parents' activities in the leisure market … Therefore the master plan was to try to make Newby attractive in some way or other to families with children, within a framework that was acceptable to the family that lived here.

'It's not Chatsworth. It's not Blenheim. It's not a huge great palace,' Richard points out, 'so what you do here can be very intrusive.'

By this stage Newby had already been open to the public for twenty years, after Robin's father opened the doors in the early 1950s, albeit on a much smaller scale than today. 'It really kept him going,' Robin maintains. 'It was very amateurish, but it was very attractive to the public. Here was a man who loved his own house and garden, taking his hat off to greet the public and parking the cars by waving his handkerchief towards their space.'

'It was great fun in those days,' Robin recalls. 'I remember sticking posters on York Station – no one stopped me – saying "Come and visit Newby half-a-crown".'

In the first year of business no more than a couple of thousand people accepted the invitation, though numbers were to grow steadily.

Robin had to be careful 'not to tread on his father's toes', even though he could see that Newby had to change in order to survive. 'This was his home still, a private home,' he emphasises. 'The public used to come in and go past the ante-room where he had his drinks tray and they could have helped themselves to a whisky and soda, if they wanted to. It was so amateurish, but it had infinite charm. That's why people came – in fairly few numbers – but they came.'

To encourage the numbers to grow, an Adventure Garden was created to provide somewhere safe where children could play on swings and climbing-frames, in pedalo boats and a pirates' fort. In conjunction with this the restaurant, which had previously been located in the elegant stable block, a long walk from the garden for small children, was moved to be near the Adventure Garden – all of which was designed to make the whole experience of visiting Newby more attractive to families.

This rethink also entailed creating a new visitor entrance in a central location, with a new car park and new information pavilion. Robin Compton's master plan envisaged a miniature railway running along the picturesque banks of the River Ure, from which there are marvellous views of the garden. And this was in addition to any work scheduled in the garden itself.

Thirty years on, that plan has largely been realised and the balance sheet at Newby Hall no doubt looks healthier as a result. 'We do visitor surveys, using questionnaires, so that we know if we are getting the marketing message right,' Richard Compton adds. 'Only twenty-eight per cent of our visitors specifically come to see the garden. Only thirteen per cent come specifically to see the house. For the rest it's a family day out. They'll wander round the garden and enjoy it, but they won't be gardening aficionados and they certainly won't be house aficionados.'

These statistics are revealing and they point to the challenge facing Richard Compton and everyone else working to build visitor numbers in historic houses. 'There are so many more activities now for the family than there were fifteen years ago. And there are other constraints, other demands on time, including basic things like Sunday shopping that did not exist then.'

Stuart Gill, the Administrator at Newby Hall with considerable experience of managing 'heritage' venues, comments, 'The other vagary we have to deal with is in terms of what we have created here – and we'll never get away from it – an outdoor attraction, with the gardens and Adventure Garden, and we are constantly at the mercy of the weather.'

This is why Newby Hall, like so many other historic houses, has joined the lucrative wedding venue and corporate hospitality market. As Stuart Gill explains, 'It effectively spreads the risk. One of these days we're going to hit the bonanza when we get a really good summer as well as a heap of corporate events – then we'll be quids in.'

That was not the case in 2006, however, when the income from corporate events only just balanced the shortfall in visitor income caused by lacklustre August weather. Furthermore, all this commercial activity has had to be achieved while retaining

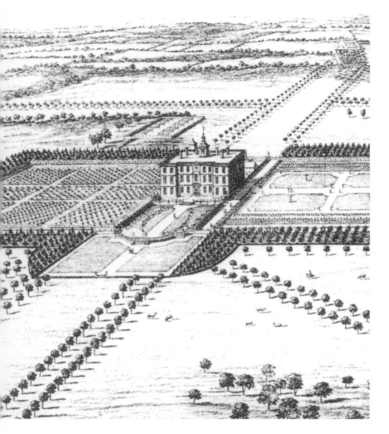

The eighteenth-century Kip drawing of Newby Hall gardens, originally designed by Peter Aram in the late seventeenth century, illustrates the complexity of its original conception. Whilst the design and style has altered with changing fashions, continuity is provided by the enthusiasm for gardening shown by recent generations.

the essential appeal of the house and gardens, without which there wouldn't be a visitor business in the first place.

The first gardens laid out at Newby Hall were typical of the formal gardens and parks designed at the end of the seventeenth century. There was an enormous orchard to the north of the house, and four square grass plots with statues to the south. Radiating from the house, avenues of lime trees pointed in different directions – one of them on a beeline for Ripon Cathedral.

This was the plan of Newby that the traveller Celia Fiennes recorded in her diary *A Journey to the North*, dating from 1697. 'A fine place of Sir Edward Blackett [the builder and first owner of Newby Hall],' she noted, 'it looks finely in the approach in the midst of a good parke and a river runs by it, it stands in the middle and has two large Gardens on each side. Fine gravel walks between the grass plots 4 square with Statues great and small in each Square, and full of borders of flowers; on the other side of the house is just such a Garden, only the walks are all grass rowl'd, and the Squares are full of dwarfe trees both fruites and green, set cross wayes which looks very finely; there is a Flower Garden behind the houses. This was the finest house I saw in Yorkshire.'

Two centuries later, Newby Hall reflected the fashion of late Victorian gardening as Robin Compton explains in his guide to the gardens: 'When my father came to Newby he wisely made careful notes and I quote from them: "I found I had inherited an exceptionally beautiful home but no garden to speak of – a lovely picture but no frame."

'The garden he saw around him consisted of two Victorian parterre gardens near the house, a large kitchen garden 400 yards (365m) away to the south-east, the Rock Garden [also constructed in the nineteenth century], equally far away to the south-west, and Burges' [nineteenth-century] statue walk linking them from east to west. The rest was rough grass, a few magnificent trees and wind – lots of it!'

'My father was a dear, lovely man,' Mr Compton senior recalls affectionately. 'He wasn't a businessman; he had no business training. He had lots of lovely dreams and he was a wonderful

draughtsman and laid out a superb plan – a grand design – and it all fitted, with a lovely sense of proportion and balance.'

His father's first task was to tackle the winds, which sweep across the Newby estate from the south and west, and in the early 1920s he planted extensive screens of trees, 'a lot of false cypresses, which I have now had to cut down because they got too old for their allotted space,' Robin Compton points out.

'He was quite right,' he adds. 'You cannot garden in a very windy site. And this was in the days when every plant in the herbaceous borders [for which Newby Hall is justifiably famous] had to be individually staked.'

The two Victorian parterre gardens jarred with the Queen Anne architecture of the house and were removed, although the pattern of their outline can still be seen in the lawns now covering the site when the weather is exceptionally dry, as it was in the early summer of 2006.

Robin Compton's description continues, 'The magnificent view to the south was central to the

Stately **Gardening**

design and became the main axis to the garden. Double herbaceous borders were planted to run straight down to the river, backed by bold hedges of yew. Off this central axis, compartmented gardens of formal design were planned, each to come into flower at different seasons.'

This provided the canvas on which Mr Compton's father worked for more than fifty years, adding

rare and beautiful plants to the gardens, which, in his son's words, 'have undeniably made a great contribution to twentieth-century garden design'.

'I was not a gardener at all when I was a child,' he

continues. 'I was keen, as most boys are, on sport, and doing a bit of hard work too; gardening came in at a later stage.'

It was after the Second World War that his interest began to take root, coupled with the knowledge that he would be inheriting Newby at some stage in the future and therefore ought to know something about gardening. So he enrolled on a correspondence course and spent a year working on a fruit farm in Worcestershire to gain some practical experience.

It was the best part of thirty years later that Robin and his wife Jane took on the responsibility of looking after Newby Hall. 'She did a lot, Janey,' her husband is happy to explain. 'She's got a very good artistic eye. We work very much as a team and together we had the conceptions and dreams of what we would like it to be. But it was her voice that first said, "This is a wonderful garden, but it's much too masculine. It hasn't had the feminine touch."'

A generation earlier, it had been Robin's father who had had the dreams. He named one of the

Sylvia's Garden, Newby Hall.

gardens he created Sylvia's Garden as a tribute to his wife, but it was his direction exclusively that guided the shape and design of the Newby Hall gardens during his lifetime.

As he grew older, though, he was unable to maintain this level of close supervision. Trees and shrubs became overgrown, matured and died off, added to which was the universal question of staffing numbers. In the 1930s twelve people had been employed at Newby to look after the garden alone; when Robin Compton and his wife took them over, the gardening team had dropped to five.

'The framework of my father's design could hardly be faulted,' Robin Compton writes, 'so the main challenge for us was to simplify the garden for ease of maintenance and to replant it with our own favourite plants.'

His wife completely redecorated the inside of the house, 'so she had a very good idea of colour, balance and light coming in and how it reflects,' Robin says. 'All of that was very helpful to me. I have the knowledge of plants and on the whole it worked very well as a combined effort.'

They introduced a number of practical measures to simplify the work, notably the use of netting set two feet above the soil and stretched the length of the herbaceous borders, which alleviates the need for individual staking. Even so Mrs Compton still needed ten years to complete the enormous task of replanting these borders that are probably Newby's best-known feature.

'Over the last decades new vistas have been created,' concludes her husband, '– glades through clumps of acers and white-barked birches, fountains streams and ponds,' all of which constitute the element of romance that marks four decades of loving care and innovation that the present owner's parents have devoted to Newby Hall. Close to the Garden Restaurant two beds of late-flowering roses are shaped in the letters R and J to mark their ruby wedding – a fitting tribute to all that they have achieved together.

Gardens, such as Newby, play an important part in conserving native species under the auspices of The National Council for the Conservation of Plants & Gardens (NCCPG), which was established in 1978. A quarter of a century later there are approaching 650 NCCPG approved National Plant Collections, nearly half of them in private ownership, preserving more than 50,000 garden plants for future generations. Since 1988, when Robin Compton was chairman of the NCCPG, Newby has been home to the National Collection of Cornus, which thrive in the well-drained sandy loam and beneath the light shade of the trees. Elsewhere there are several sizeable collections of other plants, not NCCPG collections but of great interest all the same. These include forty different specimens of magnolias, seventy-eight rhododendrons, 148 roses and thirty-four salvias.

A few miles away, the garden at Ripley Castle has the National Hyacinth Collection, which receives forty or so unusual species of hyacinth every year, courtesy of the International Bulb Centre in the Netherlands. These are planted out and come into bloom at the end of the first week in April, perfuming the garden with their glorious scent until the end of May. When the bulbs have died back, they are dug up, dried and sent for further propagation in Cambridge.

In addition to the collection of hyacinths growing outside in the gardens at Ripley, the hothouses there contain a collection of tropical plants rescued in 1991 from the disused Cottingham

As with several other owners the Ingilbys at Ripley Castle have been awarded National Collection status for their hyacinth display which adds interest to the garden in late spring.

Botanical Gardens in Hull. This brings the hothouses full circle to their Victorian heyday, and visitors today can see oranges and grapefruit growing once again at Ripley along with glorious ferns, crotons, bromeliads and a Bird of Paradise plant. There is the further benefit of providing visitors with a twelve-month asset in the gardens, which is important because Sir Thomas Ingilby is looking to open Ripley Castle to the public twelve months of the year.

In recent years the gardens at Ripley Castle, like those in many historic houses, have provided the setting for outdoor theatre productions; at Ripley they take place over three weeks beginning in the second half of June. These productions started in 2005 and take the form of a promenade event, as Sir Thomas Ingilby explains: 'People bring their own chairs and rugs, and they actually move around with the players to five or six settings in different parts of the gardens. That has worked really well.'

With a maximum audience of 150 a night, ticket sales in just the second year reached 3,000. The company was started by a couple of young professional actors, one of whom lives on the edge of the Ripley estate. 'She and her father came to me one day,' Sir Thomas continues, 'and said that they had put together a successful production somewhere in the Lake District and thought they could do one here … They really wanted to give it a go. I said it wasn't going to cost us anything and I didn't particularly expect any money at the end of it, but they amazed themselves and me by giving me a small amount of money when they finished.'

Using a number of locations in the garden certainly adds something to the performances. 'I'll never forget last year,' Sir Thomas says by way of example. 'We actually went to see *A Midsummer Night's Dream* on Midsummer Night. It was a glorious sunny evening and in the last act the sun was filtering through the trees in the woodland and it was spectacular because you could smell the woodland, you could hear the birds – it really brought Shakespeare to life. I think that's what people enjoy.'

Of course the gardens at many historic houses provide an attractive setting for wedding receptions and these too have had an impact on the planting schemes. Owners like Sir Brooke

Properties that promote themselves as wedding venues are keen to ensure all-year-round interest in their gardens, as is the case at Loseley Park.

Boothby and Sir Thomas Ingilby need to ensure that their gardens have colour throughout the year. Where in years gone by the colour might have moved from bed to bed with the seasons, these days it is important to present weddings parties with a colourful display throughout the gardens.

'Inevitably you start to concentrate on the snowdrops, the aconites and the daffodils to make sure that you have early colour,' Sir Thomas explains. 'Then in the autumn you are looking for foliage with reds and oranges in them – so it does affect the planting schemes.'

Like most other aspects of running the Castle and estate at Ripley, gardening is a skill that the Ingilbys are learning as they go along. 'The garden is more my wife's domain,' Sir Thomas will tell you. 'But she wouldn't regard herself as an expert gardener by any means. She gardens very much by colours, a bit like interior design, which actually is quite a good way of designing things.'

Garden innovation that appeals to visitors can take many forms and can come from wholly unexpected quarters. The gardening broadcaster Alan Titchmarsh was filming at Loseley Park in Surrey in 2005 and was looking round the gardens afterwards with Michael More-Molyneux, when they came across the two-and-half-acre meadow, which had formerly been planted out as a pick-it-yourself fruit operation, that lies on the other side of the moat from the gardens.

He asked what was going to happen there and Michael answered that they were thinking of planting an arboretum. 'No,' said Alan Titchmarsh, 'what you want to do is plant a wild flower meadow.'

'So, we did and we have,' Michael continues, 'and in February there were masses of weeds just queuing up to take over. Then, to our astonishment, in May, things began to turn white, blue, red and yellow and suddenly you felt you were in the Swiss mountains again. It was so exciting.'

Now there are plans to build a Monet-type bridge to link the gardens with the wild flower meadow, so that people will be able to walk through that as well.

The gardens at Loseley are not alone in lending themselves to suiting many outdoor events. 'Functions held in the garden are always a delight,' beams Michael. 'We had a Conservative drinks party one lunchtime a couple of weeks ago for the local area. That was followed by the Cancer Research Jazz Evening on the same day. We had a garden show last weekend for about 12,000. Then on Monday we had an annuals' plant

The White Garden at Loseley Park.

viewing: a walk round with the head gardener with a glass of wine and a chance to chat to him. We do wedding receptions in the garden, of course, and dinner parties.'

Does he, does every family that opens their gardens to visitors, miss the privacy that the rest of us take for granted when we settle down outside at home?

Michael More-Molyneux's reply could have come from any number of people in his position. 'The first, essential, point is that in order to do this job you've got to enjoy people; if you don't, you're in trouble up to your neck. We're not the sort of family that is looking to lie in the sun every Saturday or Sunday afternoon. In actual fact, Sarah and I will sometimes go and sit in the Walled Garden in the evening with a glass of wine and just enjoy it.

'If you're up early in the morning and in the garden at half-past six, it makes you think "My gosh, we're privileged to be able to walk out into this." One is jolly fortunate. So not necessarily being able to make use of the garden in the way in which you'd like to is not a negative.'

The pleasure owners of historic houses take from their gardens appears to be little altered from the joy their predecessors knew. In fact, present-day pleasure may be that much greater in the knowledge that the gardens that were once the exclusive preserve of the owning family and their close associates are now enjoyed by millions of people every year.

The final word should rightly come from Robin Compton – a leading gardener of his generation, widely acclaimed for his knowledge and expertise, as well as the custodian of Newby Hall, where he and his wife have created one of the country's most celebrated gardens.

'The cost of restoring and maintaining the house, gardens and all these attractions is enormous and continues to rise,' he writes in conclusion to his garden guide. 'There is often little or no profit in what we do except in the knowledge that we give great pleasure to an increasing number of visitors. '…without your help Newby could not survive as a living example of our wonderful heritage.'

Robin Compton at home in the garden he and his wife created at Newby Hall.

Secret Gardens

The First World War marked a watershed for the gardens of great houses up and down the country. The large bands of garden staff, who had tended them and brought them to their Victorian and Edwardian zenith a century ago, left the carefully prepared soil of home to battle in the mud of the Western Front and few of them ever returned to the gardens they had nurtured and loved.

In their absence, nature was given free rein. Neatly trimmed hedges blossomed into stately trees, casting a shade beneath which flowers could no longer grow. Perfectly manicured gardens, of which it could truthfully have been said before 1914 that among all the rare plants, the rarest was a weed, were quickly overwhelmed by the invasion of robust and rampant native species hungry to reclaim their old domain. Acres of glasshouses where exotic fruits had formerly been grown, sometimes at close to ruinous expense, fell into disrepair and ultimately disappeared in heaps of rotting frames and broken glass. Expansive kitchen gardens that had regularly produced

this. In the middle of the eighteenth century, when the naturalistic style of landscape gardening epitomised by 'Capability' Brown was all the rage, *The World* magazine published an article on gardens, in which the reader was informed that they 'are usually new-created once in twenty or thirty years, and no traces left of their former condition'. There was nothing peculiar or unsettling about this, the piece continued: 'Were any man of taste not to lay out his ground in the style which prevailed less than half a century ago, it would occasion as much astonishment and laughter, as if a modern beau should appear in the drawing-room in red stockings.'

fruit and vegetables of prize-winning dimensions and shape, in addition to supplying year-round provisions for households of several dozen people, became redundant when domestic staff left with the gardeners to serve King and Country. Kitchen gardens that did survive were significantly scaled down; others were grassed over or left to the whim of nature.

Yet this bleak catalogue of decline and loss does not show the whole picture. Gardens can change for other, perfectly laudable and understandable, reasons – changes of fashion and function being the most obvious – and there is nothing new in

Professional gardeners taking tremendous pride in the variety and quality of their produce.

At some historic houses the gardens that had graced them in previous centuries disappeared for good. At others they were sympathetically modified to reflect new tastes and requirements. Then there were those where vestiges of what had once existed hinted at what might be retrievable. The challenge in many cases amounts to a lifetime's work, but the rewards of recovering and restoring the secrets of the lost gardens of these historic houses are now enjoyed by hundreds of thousands of visitors as well as the owning families who have toiled in them for years aided by a handful of equally enthusiastic helpers.

In 1996 Sir Hugh and Lady Stucley inherited Hartland Abbey – the twelfth-century Stucley family home on the Atlantic coast of north Devon, a few miles south of Hartland Point and a few miles north of the Cornish border – and, in Lady Stucley's words, 'quite frankly didn't know where to begin. It was obvious that the Abbey, the gardens and the surrounding parkland were in dire need of attention but with such a huge area where should we start?'

The task that faced them mirrors a story familiar to many of the present generation of historic house owners. Restoration work in the gardens had been initiated by Sir Hugh's parents, in the case of Hartland in the 1950s and 1960s, but this had tailed off as they had grown older. Lady Stucley takes up the story, 'but with a very small gardening staff – one gardener – a lot of children to educate, very little money and huge death duties, the garden was not a huge priority … Sir Dennis [her father-in-law] died in 1983 and as Lady Stucley became older, again the garden went into decline and a succession of useless employees left their mark, including buried fridges in the Walled Gardens!'

The knowledge that three generations earlier there had been wonderful gardens to enjoy at Hartland Abbey, coupled with the excitement of rediscovering them and the prospect of sharing what was found and restored with growing numbers of visitors, inspired a decade of relentless hard work.

History laid down a marker, as Lady Stucley explains: 'The earliest gardens at the Abbey were planted by the monks in the 1100s but nothing remains of these. The gardens as they are today were planted in the eighteenth and nineteenth centuries and had been in their prime from the end of the nineteenth century up until the First World War. Much of the inspiration behind them came from Gertrude Jekyll who was a great friend of Christine Hamlyn, the owner of neighbouring Clovelly Court. Mrs Hamlyn was the sister of Marion Stucley and when Jekyll was staying at Clovelly Court they would come over to Hartland Abbey and help plan new areas of the garden with Lady Stucley. In the woodland gardens they developed winding paths, a bog garden, a fernery and in the Walled Gardens some small Italian terraces. When all the gardeners left for the Front in 1914, never to return, the gardens fell into decline. With the mild climate of Hartland and the terrible Atlantic gales sweeping up the valley from

the sea, much of the garden simply disappeared under fallen trees, brambles and ponticum rhododendrons …

'Hartland Abbey lies across a narrow, wooded valley running east to west … ending at a very wild, rocky Atlantic cove. Woodland gardens were planted on either side of the valley with a rhododendron walk, the Ladies Walk, leading to the Walled Gardens. These were built in the eighteenth century in a warm, south-facing gulley, to be sheltered from the Atlantic gales, which they are not! …'

This was the predicament that Sir Hugh and Lady Stucley faced a decade ago when they set out to reveal what nature had contrived to obscure for three-quarters of a century. 'Every day we pulled brambles and nettles and cleared fallen trees,' Lady Stucley continues. 'Parts of the woodland gardens appeared that we didn't know existed. Our second son, Peter, had three months after university before joining the army; he was hugely enthusiastic and worked really hard, and it was he who made the first most significant discovery of the paved winding paths and an old rockery

completely hidden under huge brambles, ponticum and leafmould. Also totally hidden was a twisted and gnarled acer, strangled by ivy, but so beautiful. This was the moment that we decided that we must go on. Sir Hugh and a friend then found a huge pit – the brambles hiding it had gone almost twenty feet into the trees – which turned out to be the Victorian fernery with its steps nearly intact. All summer he worked to clear it. None of this was known to the family and it was all a great surprise. Since then we have found dogs' gravestones, gazebos and many, many, more paths. Our visitors now love this secret and exciting part of the garden.'

However, Hartland Abbey had even more to offer than this. Half a mile east of the house stand the Walled Gardens, originally five separate gardens but ten years ago lost beneath a tangle of 'bindweed, ground elder, buried fridges and many other horrors'. However, as Lady Stucley and her husband were to discover, 'they did contain many old treasures: 150-year-old wisteria, a huge chimonathus, wonderful hydrangeas, roses, eucalyptus, magnolias, azaleas, bulbs and some exceptional raspberries – all needing desperate attention. After a year of sleepless nights wondering what to do, I decided that they would be such an asset to the opening of the house that we simply had to restore them. Also, I couldn't live with the knowledge that we had finally let them go. My husband thought otherwise: that we should let them to someone to market garden or preferably to keep pigs or chickens in, but essentially to bring in rent! I won and I think after years of hard slog and many more sleepless nights we are both enormously happy with the result and we have lots of kind visitors who make it feel worthwhile.'

Rediscovering the Woodland Gardens almost single-handed was hard enough, but once cleared, maintenance became a constant battle. 'After the huge task of clearing them,' continues Lady Stucley, 'each year the seeds of bramble germinate and we have to be very vigilant otherwise in no time they would be lost again. Vegetation in this part of England is very fast growing due to the mild climate. We have an ongoing battle with bamboo and Japanese

Knotweed, once so fashionable and probably brought to the garden by Jekyll. But what Victorian gardeners did not realise was how invasive they would become.'

Help also came to Hartland Abbey in the form of 'a very frail-looking twenty-one-year-old girl who had asthma, not an ideal recipe for someone to pioneer and restore a very dilapidated and weed-infested garden. However, she did come with a wonderful reference from Michael Hickson, the head gardener for many years at Knightshayes, and how grateful we are to him. Joanna Mitchell is now in her seventh year with us and thanks to her dogged determination, hard work, utter oblivion to the dreadful winter weather at Hartland (salt-laden gale force winds, tipping rain and grey, damp days) we now have a garden which delights visitors and makes an added attraction.

'Many of the plants in the garden have been given to us or we have grown from seed; our outgoings have had to be kept to a minimum. Some plants have just arrived! *Echium pininana*, the giant echium growing to twenty feet, had not been seen in the garden for fifteen years until we dug the borders again; the seed had lain dormant for all that time. They now seed themselves all over the place and are a great wow factor for visitors. As long as they don't get blown away in the winter and we don't get a hard frost for days on end, they flourish in our climate.

'We were lucky that most of the walls were intact, but they need continual patching ... The arched doorways are very pretty. Most of the glasshouses had either been blown away or were dilapidated, but in the last two years, with our own labour, we have managed to restore two of them and they now contain some tropical plants and all the many geraniums with which we decorate the Abbey for the visitors in the summer. Up until then all these plants had lived precariously under collapsing roofs; they look much happier now, as does Joanna.

'In the autumn of 2004 we received a grant from the Countryside Stewardship scheme to restore a gazebo which was totally lost under gorse, bracken and blackthorn; this will now be another attraction for the visiting public to enjoy. It is in a stunning situation overlooking the Atlantic and

was built in the late 1800s.' Sir Hugh and Lady Stucley have applied for a civil wedding licence for this tiny but eccentric building.

'There is so much more we long to do: restoring the old garden outhouses and old farm buildings in the park; restoring miles of park railings; oak trees need planting – the list goes on, but we will do what we can manage to keep up. We all work as hard as we can. We are passionate about Hartland, to us it is the most magical place in England. We just need lots of visitors to come and see what we are doing in this very special corner of the country.'

Garden history appears to be so well documented in Britain, with so many fine examples of gardens reflecting the style and tastes of particular centuries, that it's challenging to think that thirty years ago a previously unfamiliar school of garden design, the Rococo Garden, began to be unearthed and rediscovered for the first time in 250 years. Like the moraine left behind by retreating glaciers, elements of it had survived as quaint anachronisms, surrounded by the landscaped

vistas and elaborate parterres of later centuries. However, no known rococo garden had survived for scholars to study and gardeners to enjoy. It took an exhibition of paintings by the eighteenth-century artist Thomas Robins to stimulate interest in this brief period of garden evolution.

Robins's work forms the only record of rococo gardens in England. This is partly explained by the relatively short span of its popularity – a mere forty years from 1720 to 1760 – either side of which lay more familiar garden designs: the formal, regular gardens laid out close to the houses they complemented, which characterised the early eighteenth century, and the English landscape garden perfected by 'Capability' Brown, which dominated its latter half.

Squeezed between these, the rococo garden marked a transitional period of frivolity and entertainment; the name 'rococo' derives from the French words *rocaille* ('rock work') and *coquille* ('shell') – an allusion to the artfully arranged groups of rocks, sea shells and other natural forms that characterised the mood.

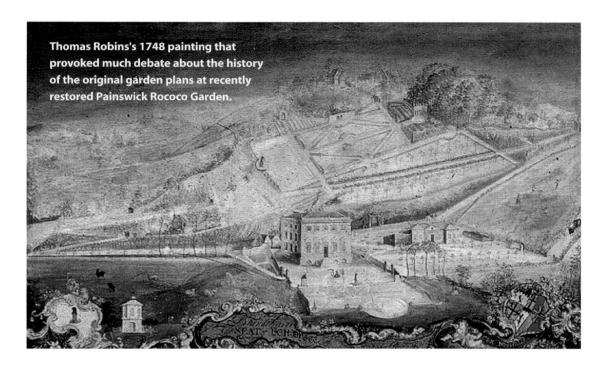

Thomas Robins's 1748 painting that provoked much debate about the history of the original garden plans at recently restored Painswick Rococo Garden.

Among Thomas Robins's paintings was one of the garden at Painswick in Gloucestershire. The owner, Benjamin Hyett, chose to create his new garden in a hidden valley behind the family home, Painswick House, rather than in front of it. This was the garden represented in Robins's painting; but whether it was a design proposal for a garden, or a representation of the garden itself, no one could tell. For, thirty years ago, the hidden valley Robins had depicted was filled with trees planted in the mid-1960s, augmented by a tangled jungle of brambles and old man's beard.

A visit by garden historians suggested that the site was worth investigating and, with a projected budget of £100,000, work started in October 1984 to recreate (as opposed to restore) Hyett's garden, with his descendant Lord Dickinson footing the bill.

Not far into the project, Paul Moir, a member of the owning family, started working at Painswick, after developing a career in marketing. He still manages the garden today and has therefore been involved in the work at Painswick for most of its evolution.

The initial work required the removal of the recent woodland, clearing fallen trees, regravelling paths, draining and repuddling the main fish pond and undertaking some preliminary work on what remained of the garden buildings. However, it soon became apparent that the original costing was wholly inadequate and that continuing with the work privately was wholly unrealistic. So in 1988 the Painswick Rococo Garden Trust became a registered charity to carry on the work.

'About that time,' Paul Moir explains, 'something else happened that increased the costs drastically. We were approached by Bath Archaeological Trust to do an archaeological dig to see if there was any evidence of the original garden. In other words,

could we confirm it was a painting of the actual garden or a proposal for it?'

What the archaeologists found showed that there was significant evidence that the garden had been created as Robins depicted it and that his painting was therefore a picture of the actual garden at Painswick. The consequences of this discovery were far-reaching. These revelations established Painswick as the only surviving complete rococo garden in the country and consequently switched the work from 'recreating' what might have been there, to 'restoring' what had actually been there.

'This put a lot more financial obligations on us,' Paul Moir continues. 'Where we started putting buildings back, we did it authentically; rather than using a glass-fibre screen [for the Gothic-screened exedra] we used oak laths and plaster ... It also meant that before we started rushing in to do something, we had to check first what was there. That put the costs up ...

'The main problem of the route we have gone down is that not only are the restoration costs

A wonderful example of rococo architectural
frivolity that is still integral to the existing
garden design at Painswick.

more expensive, but the maintenance costs are astronomical. In 1991 we restored one of the buildings in the garden [the strangely named Eagle House]. We are now having to do further restoration work on it and that is costing us £30,000 ... The exedra was first done in 1992 and last year it cost us £24,500 to do the maintenance and repair on it.'

And this was solely because of the construction materials: lath and plaster. When the buildings were first built, Paul explains, labour was cheap and the garden buildings regarded more as stage

The exedra, a curving decorative screen, at Painswick was designed to catch the eye in its location above the kitchen garden and is another example of the whimsy that typifies the rococo movement.

sets than structures that would last indefinitely; if one fell down, it was simple enough to put up another to replace it. 'The essence of the garden is that it should not to be taken seriously,' he told an interviewer. 'It is not a natural garden although the planting is loose. It is a garden designed to be used and enjoyed.'

These are not costs associated with most gardens, in which labour forms the single greatest outlay. At Painswick, however, the cost of building maintenance equates to a third of the amount spent on labour. There is no denying that these buildings are charming and contribute hugely to what Paul calls the flamboyant mood of the garden but, built as they are, they come at a price. Constructed originally as playful follies from which to admire the garden, they now provide somewhere for visitors to take a rest themselves, and in a couple of cases act as romantic locations for civil weddings to take place.

From Paul Moir's perspective, as a garden administrator trying to balance the books, projected maintenance costs of this order act as a constraint on the speed at which further

restoration can progress. 'We have reached the situation now,' he says, 'when we are almost struggling to keep the garden in the state it is in at the moment.'

Strangely enough thirty per cent of annual business at Painswick comes in February, when visitors flock to the garden to see the glorious display of snowdrops that carpet the whole valley. The irony is not lost on Paul Moir, who acknowledges, 'We are very reliant on something that is wholly irrelevant to the history of the garden.'

Add to this the constant struggle to draw visitors who have so many other attractions and distractions to occupy their time, and the need to focus on providing a place of relaxation and 'entertainment' counts far more in the success or failure of the garden than solely providing a rarified site of archaeological, historical or even horticultural significance.

The same pragmatic considerations led to the creation in 1998 of a maze that marked the 250th anniversary of Thomas Robins's painting and also provided a hugely popular visitor attraction. To

The wonderful snowdrop display at Painswick paradoxically provides a source of income quite unrelated to its restored garden and at a time of the year when visitors are thin on the ground.

The Plunge Pool at Painswick provided a bracing dip for eighteenth-century dandies.

avoid detraction from the restoration, this was deliberately planted outside the area of the garden shown in the painting; although it does help remove 'the seriousness of gardening', as Paul Moir sees it, thereby reflecting the underlying spirit that inspired the creation of the Painswick Rococo Garden in the first place.

Pragmatism led to the restoration of the large kitchen garden, where fruit and vegetables served in the restaurant are grown – where possible these are varieties that would have been grown here in the eighteenth century. The same goes for the hydraulic ram, which has been removed from the Ram House at the corner of the Fish Pond and is awaiting restoration. The ram, powered by nothing other than the natural flow of water, was originally used to pump water to great heights. Water flowing from the Plunge Pool down to the Fish Pond provided the power to pump water to the tanks in the attics of Painswick House. Only the gentle 'thumping' in the background gave an indication of what was happening and one day, as money and need dictate, that sound may be heard again, bringing a further reminder of what it might have been like to stroll around this particular Cotswold gem two-and-a-half centuries ago.

Painshill Park near Cobham in Surrey has a name very similar to the rococo garden at Painswick, while the original layout dates from the same period in the middle of the eighteenth century. Like Painswick Rococo Garden, Painshill fell into decay after the Second World War and might have been lost for good had it not been for the foresight of Elmbridge Borough Council, who bought the 158-acre estate in 1980 and a year later established the Painshill Park Trust to restore and preserve the landscape, lake, plantings and buildings.

Painshill has been described as one of the most important eighteenth-century parks in Europe. It was the creation of a young nobleman, Charles Hamilton, who having completed his Grand Tour returned to England and set about creating a garden that would stir the emotions of all who saw it. Hamilton's own emotions had evidently been stirred by the lavish cascades and highly decorative grottoes he had seen on his European travels, and by the haunting classical landscapes depicted in the paintings of eighteenth-century artists such as Poussin and Claude Lorraine. He began by leasing a strip of land on the edge of a moor near the River Mole and with money borrowed from friends (the family coffers were insufficient for his plans) commenced the design of what amounted to a theatrical landscape.

One of Hamilton's first steps was to create a thirty-acre serpentine lake fed by water from the Mole, and then he began on the building. There was a wood, plaster and papier-mâché Temple of Bacchus, the carefully constructed ruins of an 'abbey', a Gothic temple, a Turkish tent, a crystal grotto, a Gothic tower, a Chinese bridge and more. Hamilton also spent large sums of money on the planting. Many new and rare shrubs were introduced and it was said that Painshill had the most varied collection of conifers in the world.

There was only one thing missing. It had become rather fashionable to have a hermitage and, of course, Hamilton had built a rather splendid one complete with an upstairs sleeping chamber. The only problem was that the Hermitage lacked a

The Pigeon House – the only functional building in the garden at Painswick.

hermit. An advertisement was placed and perhaps not surprisingly there was not a lot of interest.

Life as a hermit was not easy. The common terms of employment were that the appointed hermit would stay in the Hermitage for seven years, 'wearing a camel-hair robe, studying the Bible, thinking great thoughts, and being civil to visitors'. It was against the rules for the hermit to leave the garden or cut his hair, beard or nails during his tenure. In return, at the end of seven years, the hermit would receive the princely sum of £700.

Hamilton did eventually find a hermit, but unfortunately he was a bit of a beer drinker and as alcohol was strictly forbidden it proved to be something of a stumbling block. Within the month Hamilton found his 'hermit' down at the local inn and his employment was promptly terminated. In spite of various efforts to find a replacement the post remained vacant.

Under the circumstances it was probably just as well as Hamilton was not really in a position to pay £100 let alone £700 to anyone. He tried a variety of schemes to make Painshill a paying concern – there

was a vineyard that produced a more than passable sparkling wine – but none brought in the money needed to keep Painshill viable. In 1773 the friends who had financed Hamilton called in their loans and Hamilton had to sell up. He repaid his creditors and moved to Bath where he died thirteen years later at the age of eighty-two. In spite of his restricted means and limited space in his new home Hamilton was an avid gardener to the end and his love of Painshill never dimmed; the inventory of his possessions after his death included a large number of paintings of the park he had created.

After Hamilton had left Painshill the property passed through a number of hands and in 1948 was sold off in lots. What remained of the garden was left to its own devices until in the early 1980s the Trust was formed to save Hamilton's vision for the nation. More than twenty years of challenging and difficult work was to follow, and work scheduled for the future, when funds permit, includes constructing six features in the gardens together with completion of Hamilton's partly restored grotto. The success of what has been achieved was aptly summed by the citation in

1998, which accompanied the awarding of a rare Europa Nostra medal, that reads 'for the exemplary restoration from the state of extreme neglect, of a most important 18th-century landscape park and its extraordinary buildings'.

Even internationally renowned gardens like those at Chatsworth have hidden secrets. In the late 1980s a programme of clearing *Rhododendron ponticum*, laurel and self-sown sycamore from several acres of the Chatsworth garden led to discoveries that took even someone as well-informed about her home as the Dowager Duchess of Devonshire by surprise. 'After forty years I thought I knew the garden well,' she writes in *The Estate*, 'but the clearance was a time of discovery: paths, streams and rocks appeared which I had never seen before.'

This clearing produced unexpected finds as well, notably the Greek altar dating from the fourth century BC, which the sixth Duke had brought to Chatsworth more than a hundred years earlier.

Her son, the twelfth Duke, shares his parents' close interest in the evolution of the gardens at Chatsworth as a changing, growing environment. 'I think we can have a really good look at the garden and see what went on,' he says. Comparing it with a similar analysis of the interior of the house, he makes the point, 'It's a much softer metamorphosis from different periods of design, because it's covered in grass rather than stone …'

'Although my parents did some very important things in the 1950s, they didn't really get stuck into the far garden until the seventies and eighties,' and here the Duke sees the opportunity for further investigation.

'There are an awful lot of trees about eight inches across which I think are self-sown, because they're in odd places. So I think it would be interesting to review their on-going status and see whether it would be better to perhaps try to restore some of that to what it was – the bits we like.'

Beside his desk is a very detailed 1858 map, showing precisely how that part of the garden was laid out 150 years ago. 'If we're going to make any changes,' he continues, 'and it's irresistible to do that – it's just the best fun – it's better to be informed of what was there before you change anything.'

Two hundred and fifty years ago, close to the time when Lancelot 'Capability' Brown was transforming the garden and park at Chatsworth for the fourth Duke of Devonshire, high walls of stone brick were built round a five-acre rectangle of land just outside the small Yorkshire town of Helmsley on the southern edge of the North York Moors. Created by the Feversham family, owners of nearby Duncombe Park, the Walled Garden at Helmsley supplied all their household fruit (including pineapples, grown in the specially constructed and heated pineapple house, and grapes from the carefully tended vinery), vegetables, orchids and cut flowers for a century and a half. Come 1918 and the world of the Edwardian country house, served by phalanxes of domestic servants and garden staff, had gone for ever.

The Fevershams' huge Walled Garden at Helmsley, unsustainable and anachronistic, was let to a

Abandoned and neglected-the derelict glasshouses and beds at Helmsley Walled Garden.

Following extensive restoration the Walled Garden is returned to its former productivity.

commercial market gardener who dispensed with the ornamental beds and borders. In the Second World War they were ploughed up as part of the 'Dig for Victory' campaign. By 1954 they were abandoned altogether and over the next forty years, the fruit trees disappeared, the glasshouses collapsed, and sycamore and willow battled with brambles to establish supremacy. 'The only semblance of order,' writes Sir Thomas Ingilby in *Yorkshire's Great Houses*, 'was a small secluded area in the lee of the walls, where one enterprising local cleared a space big enough to grow several cannabis plants.'

However, the cannabis grower was not the only person to see the potential that lay hidden behind the garden walls at Helmsley. Alison Ticehurst, the wife of a local doctor, regularly drove past and was saddened at the neglect and waste. Despite being forbidden to garden by her father, who was of the firm opinion that, 'it wasn't a suitable career for a genteel lady', Alison had longed to garden on a grand scale. After her father's death, she wasted little time in putting her plan into practice and leased the gardens from the estate in 1994. With what Sir Thomas admiringly describes as 'terrifying passion and vigour', Alison sold her substantial home and moved into a small cottage near the garden, in order to plough the sizeable balance from the sale into restoring the gardens.

Where she led, others quickly followed and when her own funds were used up, the Helmsley Walled Garden Trust was created to carry on the work. When Alison Ticehurst died in the spring of 1999, most of the garden had been cleared, the paths had been reinstated, some of the greenhouses had been restored and the first of the newly established flowerbeds were 'maturing nicely'.

By this time Alison Ticehurst's enthusiasm and commitment had been matched by that of Paul Radcliffe, who had been so captivated by the work of the 'crazy gardening woman' he had heard about, that he left his native Manchester and his salaried (though highly stressful) job running the horticultural department of a technical college and set up home in Helmsley to commit himself to the Walled Garden. 'It was completely illogical,' he is candid enough to admit. 'At least I had a steady income at the tech. Here the future was anything but secure, and the whole thing could and probably should have ended in disaster.'

But it didn't and it hasn't. By his own estimation it could take another twenty-five years to achieve all that he would like to in bringing the garden back to life. Far from being daunted by the task, Paul seems to relish the prospect, 'When I lived in Manchester I was surrounded by millions of people – but I was lonely. Helmsley's population just about runs to 1,600, but it's a real community and everyone looks after each other. I can honestly say that I haven't looked back.'

The garden now employs three full-time gardeners, who are helped by over thirty volunteers 'aged eighteen to eighty' whose passion for the Walled Garden is every bit as strong as Paul's.

Restoration aside, the gardens are also repaying the years of loving care that have been spent on them by generating income in a variety of ways. Working in association with the British Clematis Society, there are now over 200 different varieties of Clematis grown at Helmsley Walled Garden, enabling it to provide the most comprehensive collection in the UK. An extensive range of plants is available for sale, including many unusual varieties. Cut flowers and flowers for drying are sold too, as are fruit and vegetables in season. The newly restored Victorian Vinery houses the garden's café where patrons can enjoy plants and vegetables fresh from the garden.

But the range of enterprises is not restricted to garden produce. In the shop you can find a wide selection of items, the majority of which are made locally, covering everything from bags and bird boxes to pottery, preserves and wool fat soap.

A dozen years after Alison Ticehurst set to cutting back the tangled mesh of undergrowth and nettles that clogged the five acres enclosed by stately walls, the metamorphosis at Helmsley Walled Garden is remarkable. In place of weeds and illicit cannabis plants, scented borders, rose beds and a peony garden have been created alongside the areas allocated to growing fruit and vegetables. One million pounds has been spent on restoring the Vinery Orchard house, the shop and outbuildings, and 40,000 visitors come every year to enjoy the beauty and tranquility that Alison Ticehurst sensed lay hidden there, waiting

to be discovered and brought back to productive life once again.

Many historic houses with sizeable estates are faced with similar dilemmas. Gardens and parklands that were confidently laid out two and a half centuries ago when labour was plentiful and cheap, became impossible to maintain in the harsher economic climate of the twentieth century. It says a great deal for the present generation of owning families that in so many cases they are developing a range of estate-based businesses, which are providing funds to pay for the gradual restoration and preservation of historic features of their estates, along with the upkeep of their houses and the collections they contain.

Powderham Castle, overlooking the estuary of the River Exe in Devon, is the home of the Earl and Countess of Devon, who have been very active in undertaking a range of restoration and conservation projects. These have had to be carefully staged, as Lord Devon writes in his monograph on running a modern estate, which appears in the Castle guide. 'As with most estates without large fortunes to exhaust, the position remains that … Powderham barely generates enough revenue to ensure continued long-term survival in the face of increased maintenance costs, increased intervention by national and local government, and capital taxation.'

He also explains that, 'Income from the visitor enterprise coupled with Countryside Commission grants have enabled us to undertake a massive project to restore and reopen the eighteenth-century Woodland Gardens, the Belvedere Tower and the enormous walled garden, in which all the estate's fruit and vegetables traditionally were grown.'

The Woodland Garden was created in the eighteenth century by the third Viscount Courtenay and was stocked with a wide range of exotic species – from the Americas and other parts of the world – in order to achieve a lush leafy glade where the third Viscount and his sisters enjoyed elaborate picnics. Within a generation, though, the gardens had become neglected and remained so for close to 200 years until Lord Devon began to clear and restore them in 1994.

New trees have been planted to replace those that had reached maturity, shrubs that had grown into thickets have been thinned and new ones planted to establish new growth in the garden. The Mill Leat that runs along the bottom of the Woodland Garden has been cleared and now runs over the spillway as it once did. Emergency repairs have saved the Regency summerhouse from deteriorating further and a full restoration is planned when further funds become available.

The Belvedere was constructed for the second Viscount in 1773 and, set on a prominent hill, extended the scenic possibilities of the estate. Designed as a pseudo-Gothic tower, the Belvedere was admired as a romantic landscape object in its own right; once again the third Viscount and his sisters made good use of it for dances and picnics. In the 1830s it was converted into two-storey accommodation. However, two post-war fires gutted the building entirely, leaving a bare shell, and so it might have remained but for the advent of mobile phones and the need to find suitably discreet locations for signal transmission masts. The Belvedere at Powderham fitted the

The Belvedere, built as a decorative tower to embellish the grounds of Powderham and used by the third Viscount as a venue for parties, is now being used to generate income for the estate in a distinctly twenty-first-century way.

Fonmon Castle.

Stately Gardening

specification ideally and thanks to the rent paid by the company concerned and a grant from English Heritage, a three-year restoration plan has been drawn up that will see the Belvedere once again restored to its former glory.

At Fonmon Castle, Sir Brooke Boothby, aided by members of his family, has been steadily restoring and reclaiming areas of the gardens that had become run down and over-run. 'There's an area which we now call the Dell Garden,' he mentions as an example of what has been happening, 'and we're pretty certain it's the point at which a lot of the stone from which the Castle is built was dug out from the side of the bank here.' (Fonmon Castle dates from around 1200, when defence and self-protection dictated that castle walls were metres thick in places; so the Dell represents a significant excavation.) 'The woods had invaded it,' he continues. 'Ten years ago it was sycamore trees and ground elder.'

So a good deal of felling, clearing and back-breaking weeding was needed before work could begin on creating a garden in this delightful

102

hollow. One of Sir Brooke's sisters is a garden designer and she was delegated the task of coming up with a planting scheme that would suit the site – or, as her brother puts it, 'I let her loose on the operation and it's very pretty now.'

Another medieval feature of the gardens at Fonmon is a watchtower that has also been restored and restocked with doves. Fonmon, like many properties, is fortunate in having a detailed photographic record stretching well back into the nineteenth century. This shows that very little has altered in the general design of the garden; what has changed are points of small, but significant detail. For example, photographs dating from the late 1880s show a footpath curving from the house to the stable block, which is grassed over today. 'I may well restore that,' says Sir Brooke. 'It would be useful for disabled visitors to use, where now they only have grass.' The fact that photographic evidence confirms that there used to be a footpath there would lend substantial weight to obtaining planning permission to reinstate it. 'I probably wouldn't bother to put the path back for our own use,' Sir Brooke says. 'We could just as easily walk over the grass.'

With the steady flow of visitors, though, requiring firm dry surfaces to get from place to place in the gardens at Fonmon, it looks like money well spent. Restoring gardens not only brings pleasure to the families now living in historic houses – in a great many cases it brings new visitors to enjoy what has been reinstated and saved from disappearing for ever.

An old map of the Fonmon estate.

Open for Business

The gardens and parkland of historic houses have always provided entertainment in one form or another. In many cases access was not restricted to the owners of the great houses on which the surrounding grounds were centred; local villagers and farm servants, as well as visiting travellers were frequently allowed to walk the great estates and enjoy their rural delights.

Often the gardens and parklands reflect the enthusiasms and interests of their owners at different periods; and this is still the case today. From the landscaped vistas created by 'Capability' Brown to the more individual passions exhibited by the owners of some great country houses in the past, their gardens and wider grounds have provided a setting for a diverse range of activities, public and private.

Viscount Petersham, later to become the fourth Earl of Harrington, was a man with particular tastes. Something of a dandy, Charles Stanhope enjoyed clothes and it was suspected that, to look his best, he wore corsets to show them off to advantage. Distrustful of tailors, he preferred to cut out his own clothes to ensure the perfect fit and even designed a jacket – known as a Petersham – that the then Prince of Wales copied, having one made for each day of the week.

Maintaining strict sartorial standards and a spot of soldiering kept the Viscount busy until he was fifty, when within a very short space of time he inherited Elvaston Castle in Derbyshire, succeeded to the Earldom and married. The new Countess of Harrington, formerly an actress, was considerably younger than her husband and he decided to

redesign the gardens for her as a lavish wedding present. It was a project that was to last more than thirty-five years and involve more than eighty gardeners.

'Capability' Brown unfortunately declined to take on the project and it was down to the ever-patient William Barron, formerly of the Edinburgh Botanical Gardens, to meet the Earl's demands. These included planting and maintaining more than eleven miles of evergreen hedges, supervising the building of a curious temple that

has been described as being 'Sino-Moorish-quasi-Gothic', creating an Alhambra garden, a French garden, grottoes, rock gardens and countless conceits. It is not recorded what the Countess thought of her wedding gift but others have called it 'an outrageous phantasmagoria'.

In contrast to the overblown excesses in which some eighteenth-century landowners indulged, there was an earnest attempt to improve agriculture through the application of rational principles of food production and livestock

rearing. This interest in farming among the great landowners, which stemmed from the enthusiasm for agriculture shown by George II and Queen Caroline, was still strong in the early years of the nineteenth century.

The annual sheep-shearing exhibitions and festivities at Holkham Hall, in Norfolk, in 1806 were described as 'the happy resort of the most distinguished patrons and amateurs of Georgic employments'. Their host, Thomas Coke, who three decades later would be made Earl of Leicester, presided for a week over an open house in which 600 guests sat down to dinner. Hundreds of guests came from abroad, among them a representative sent by the emperor of Russia. Coke's dedication and passion for agricultural improvement bore spectacular results: between 1776 (the year in which he first represented Norfolk as a Whig MP) and 1816 the annual rent at Holkham increased almost tenfold, from £2,200 to £20,000. His efforts had an impact far beyond his own estate, however. Thanks to Coke north-west Norfolk switched from a rye-growing area to one of the richest wheat-growing regions in England, while more stock and better breeds of sheep, cattle and pigs were introduced to the county's farms.

In the following century it was a passion for wildlife conservation rather than fatstock improvement that inspired Charles Waterton of Walton Hall to stamp his mark on his family seat. A gentle, fun-loving man, he was noted at an early age for displaying a genuine love for and understanding of all animal and bird life – with the sole exception of the brown rat, a species he hated with an intense and irrational loathing.

The squire's strong attachment to the natural world gained full expression when he inherited the family estate in West Yorkshire. Rather than enhance the formal gardens and parkland, Waterton proceeded to encircle all 300 acres with a high wall to create England's first animal and bird sanctuary. The move was considered distinctly odd by his neighbours, as was Waterton's habit of inviting his guests to scale the highest trees to inspect hawks' nests and suchlike.

All animals (except, of course, brown rats) and birds were welcomed by Waterton who had a particular fondness for hedgehogs, once kept a three-toed sloth in his room and, at various stages in his life, lavished attention on a Bahia toad and a deformed duck that had been hatched on his estate.

Waterton always prided himself on his ability to endure physical hardship and after his young wife died in childbirth early on in their marriage he took to the unheated attic. He dismissed a bed as 'an absolutely useless luxury' and chose to sleep on the floor. He had a wooden pillow for his head, an old cloak for bedclothes and the windows were permanently open to allow bats and owls free entry.

When he was not off travelling – his other great passion – Squire Waterton would be up before dawn to climb his trees and study the bird life of which he kept extremely thorough and detailed accounts throughout his long life.

Climbing of any form never worried Charles Waterton, who remained amazingly supple throughout his life. (There is a report that aged seventy-seven he was still able to scratch the back of his head with the big toe of his right foot.)

The esteemed Squire of Walton Hall lived to be eighty-three and while his contemporaries thought of him as a harmless and goodly eccentric, Charles Waterton is now also considered to be one of the first great nature conservationists.

Where Waterton was something of a recluse, the nineteenth-century Lord Egremont was a landowner and employer who revelled in the company of other people, on occasions as many as possible.

His birthday each year was always celebrated by an enormous party at Petworth. Although this fell in December, Lord Egremont held his 1834 celebrations in May, because illness had prevented him staging the usual winter feast in the grounds. Charles Greville was one of the guests and described the occasion in his diary: 'A fine sight it was; fifty-four tables, each fifty feet long, were placed in a vast semi-circle on the lawn before the house. Nothing could be more amusing than to look at the preparations. The tables were all spread with cloths and plates and dishes. Two great tents were erected in the middle to receive the provisions, which were conveyed in carts like ammunition. Plum puddings and loaves were piled like cannon-balls and innumerable joints of boiled and roast beef were spread out, while hot joints were prepared in the kitchen and sent forth as the firing of a gun announced the hour of the feast. Tickets were given to the inhabitants of a certain district and the number was about four thousand, but as many more came the old peer could not endure that here should be anybody hungering outside the gates and he went out himself and ordered the barriers to be taken down and admittance given to all. They think six thousand were fed. Gentlemen from the neighbourhood carried for them and waiters were provided from among the peasantry ... a band of music paraded round. The day was glorious, an unclouded sky, a soft southern breeze, he was in and out of the windows of his rooms twenty times, enjoying the sight of these poor wretches in their best, cramming themselves and their brats with as much as they could devour and snatching a day of relaxation and happiness ... Fireworks

followed, before the day ended, ten thousand people were said to have assembled.'

Sir George Sitwell, father of the talented literary trio, Edith, Osbert and Sacheverell, was passionate about medieval history, genealogy and landscape gardening, and it was at the family seat, Renishaw Hall near Eckington in Derbyshire, that his horticultural fantasies were first played out. He was a great admirer of the classical Italianate style and vehemently opposed to anything that smacked of the Romantic. His plans for Renishaw were elaborate and, at one stage, it is claimed he employed 4,000 men to dig out an artificial lake in the grounds. (Sir George supervised their progress from precarious wooden towers that he had erected around the garden to afford him a bird's-eye view of the work in hand.)

Sitwell was forever dreaming up grand schemes and his eldest son, Osbert, once wrote of his father, 'He abolished small hills, created lakes, and particularly liked to alter the levels at which full grown trees were standing. Two old yew trees in front of the dining-room window at Renishaw, were regularly heightened and lowered; a process which I believe could have been shown to chart, like a thermometer, the temperature of his mood.'

One of Sir George's more absurd ideas (and a graphic example of why he was popularly taken to be truly eccentric) was to stencil willow pattern designs on the rumps of his herd of white cattle so as to improve their rather dull appearance. Unfortunately the experiment was short lived as the beasts refused to stay still long enough for the artist to complete the work.

Nonetheless he retained his enthusiasm for farming and once even proposed to pay Sacheverell's fees at Eton in pigs and potatoes. (The offer was declined.)

Renishaw Hall, Derbyshire.

Sir George was a great believer in his own talents and, so that the world might better appreciate the correct way to do things, in 1909 he published *On the Making of Gardens*, a book that has been described as 'an argument for imaginative thought in garden planning'. (While Sir George wrote various other books, including the *History of the Fork*, and *The Errors of Modern Parents*, his gardening tome was the only one to make it into print.)

He was a man who was constantly dreaming up new schemes and remained undeterred when some of his more bizarre ideas failed to impress. His musical toothbrush and his miniature revolver for shooting wasps may not have found general favour, but they afforded him great amusement. He would often sit out on the terrace at Renishaw taking pot shots at unsuspecting wasps 'with limited success but enormous satisfaction'.

As for gardening, it remained a passion all his life and it was one of his few pursuits that bore fruit. His gardens at Renishaw bear his stamp to this day, as do the gardens at Castello di Montegufoni, a property in the heart of Tuscany that Sir George bought in the early twentieth century to further his interest in the Italian style.

While Sir George Sitwell busied himself at Renishaw, a dozen miles to the west, the Duke of Devonshire played his part in local activities at Chatsworth. The military review that was held in the park was 'a great sight to see' according to Samuel Nunney, a public driver in the days when horses and carriages still ruled the road. The Chatsworth military review 'was watched by thousands of people, invited and uninvited, as the Duke always left the park open on all occasions'.

In the course of his work Samuel Nunney came to know many great houses, their owners and their guests. 'Several times have I met the late King Edward [VII] in Chatsworth,' he notes in his collection of reminiscences *A Life on the Road*. 'He would always salute in the old-fashioned way, and wish you Good Day. As when on a visit to the Duke at Chatsworth, any one was allowed to roam about as they liked; no protection was needed while the King was there …

'It was a pleasure to be a driver in those days,' he continues. 'I well remember seeing the late Lord Kitchener when he paid a visit to the Duke of Portland at Welbeck Abbey to speak at the Agricultural Show. I remember him receiving a telegram at that time stating that Lord Roberts had entered Pretoria in South Africa during the Boer War. That was a great day at Welbeck.

'Also I was at Welbeck when the late Joseph Chamberlain came to speak there in the riding school. It was so crowded; more like a race meeting than a private ground.'

Agricultural shows, and speciality shows catering for thousands of people continue to be held in the parks of historic houses. For the last two years the annual Darlington Dog Show has taken place in the grounds of Newby Hall over three days in the middle of September. With an estimated 15,000 dogs and owners, it is one of the major events in the canine calendar. In 2006 the show coincided with the month-long filming at Newby of a dramatisation of Jane Austen's novel *Mansfield Park*. Although most of the filming was taking place inside the house, sounds from the dog show a few hundred yards away across the park might well have made a distant unscripted contribution to any scenes shot that weekend.

The dog show at Newby Hall is the second of three major events scheduled every September. Stuart Gill, the Administrator, explains the reasoning behind this: 'We start off with the Plant Fair. We have the Darlington Dog Show. Then we have the Craft Fair. They're deliberately put there to spread the income out and also spread the workload. We're hoping in August to be attracting 1,800–2,000 people a day; so we don't want to be adding another 10,000 people to the 2,000 who

are already here. But in September we can cope with those numbers.'

The Special Events Guide for Loseley Park shows a very similar programme in September for the area of southern England that it serves. There's a Rare Plant Sale on the first Sunday in the month and a major national dog show, the Richmond Dog Show, with more than 10,000 dogs competing over three days the following weekend.

A month later, in October 2006, the National Ploughing Championships were scheduled to be held on the estate. This follows the success of the Surrey County Ploughing Match, which attracted over seventy entries the previous year. Supported by an owning family that has farmed the same fields for over 400 years, the sight of heavy horse teams ploughing the stubble fields alongside vintage tractors and the latest in agricultural machinery reflects the enormous changes that have taken place in agriculture in the last hundred years.

However, Loseley has developed this time-honoured tradition beyond a trip down memory lane. Alongside the ploughing competition has grown a country fair that draws over 10,000 spectators to a range of rural sports and activities including sheepdog trials, falconry displays, fly-fishing demonstrations, terrier racing and gundog training. All of which is a happy blend of traditional farming and country activities that reflect the particular interests of Loseley's owner, Michael More-Molyneux, who served as President of the Surrey County Agricultural Society in 2005.

Situated just a few miles from Guildford, Loseley, as its owner is quick to acknowledge, 'is in the very fortunate position that there aren't too many other sites around that can deal with over 1,000 people without any problem at all'.

Fonmon Castle, in south Wales, provides the setting every year for the Vale of Glamorgan Show, run by the Vale of Glamorgan Agricultural Society which pays 'a modest stipend' for the use of the site. 'It suits me well,' explains the Castle's owner, Sir Brooke Boothby. 'The farmers occupying the land here are mainly arable farmers and they can work around the seventy acres of grass [occupied by the show ground]. Anyhow, I want to keep seventy acres of grass to the west of the Castle as a sort of mini park.' About one year in five the heavens open and the showground is churned up by vehicles, but Sir Brooke and his tenants manage to reinstate it in time. When the show was held on its previous site, in the grounds of Sir Brooke's cousin's castle, which is also in the Vale of Glamorgan, the tenant farmer there needed good quality grass in the summer for the cattle he was rearing. Having seventy acres flattened by an agricultural show or churned up in a quagmire every few years didn't help his business, so a new home was found at Fonmon to everyone's satisfaction.

The risks posed by the British weather to elaborate outdoor events cannot be under-estimated, especially in earlier times, when temporary shelter was less advanced than it is today. In 1839 Lord Eglinton, a fervent admirer of the works of Sir Walter Scott, staged the famous

Lord Eglington
resplendent in his
suit of steel armour
inlaid with gold.

Eglinton tournament in Scotland as an evocation of medieval chivalric endeavour. During two years of meticulous planning, Lord Eglinton's enthusiasm spread among many of the younger aristocracy and a tournament worthy of Camelot captured the imagination of the well-to-do.

At £40,000, the cost of the enterprise was staggering. Huge sums were paid to acquire authentic armour from all over Europe. Eglinton himself was described as 'as handsome and gallant a knight as ever put lance in rest, resplendent in a suit of steel armour inlaid with gold, said to have cost £1,000'.

On 15 July, rehearsals for the tournament took place and *The Times* was on hand to record the proceedings:

'At four o'clock the business of the day commenced. There might be seen men in complete steel, riding with light lances at the ring, attacking the "quintain" and manoeuvring their steeds in every variety of capriole. Indeed the show of horses was one of the best parts of the sight. Trumpeters were calling the jousters to horse and the wooden figure, encased in iron panoply, was prepared for the attack. A succession of chevaliers, *sans peur et sans reproche*, rode at their hardy and unflinching antagonist, who was propelled to the combat by the strength of several stout serving-men in the costume of the olden time … The knight had certainly no easy task to perform; the weight of armour was rather heavier than the usual trappings of a modern dandy, and the heat of the sun appeared to be baking the bones of the competitors. Be this as it may, there was no flinching. The last part of the tournament consisted of the knights tilting at each other. The Earl of Eglinton … was assailed by Lord Cranston … the lances of these champions were repeatedly shivered in the attack but neither was unhorsed; fresh lances were supplied by the esquires and the sport grew fast and furious …'

Such would have been the spectacle on the day of the tournament itself had not the weather intervened. The rain poured down and tempers rose. 'In a melée of swords,' wrote one commentator, 'the Marquis of Waterford and Lord Alford distinguished themselves by losing their tempers and laying on to each other with such vigorous and lusty strokes that had they not been separated by the marshals, one or both of them would probably have been maimed for life, for both were exceptionally powerful and athletic men.'

Something rather less dramatic, though certainly more profitable, was staged at Ripley Castle a hundred years later. Outdoor historical pageants were very much in vogue in the 1930s, and the pageant held at Ripley attracted enormous audiences and raised £8,000 in two nights – enough money to build an entire wing of Harrogate hospital.

In you want an adrenalin rush at Ripley Castle these days, you can test your nerve on the high and low ropes course, 'which makes the woodland area of the garden', in Sir Thomas's words, 'part of the Castle product for corporate events'.

Created ten years ago, this venture illustrates the welcome degree of enlightened mutual self-interest that many historic house owners are showing in helping new start-up businesses on their estates: whether in redundant agricultural buildings, or, as is the case at Ripley, in part of the grounds that offered further income-producing potential.

The rope course at Ripley was created, Sir Thomas says, 'by a young couple who had been in New Zealand for their gap year. They'd seen the idea and wanted to have a go at running one here … It was a very low-input business to start with. We said they could have that area of ground [rent free] for a couple of years to see how they got on. That gave them a low overhead; it lowered the risk for them. It enabled their business to survive and prosper and in turn has brought far greater return to us … We have encouraged a lot of businesses on the estate by helping them to get started and making sure that they have as few obstacles as possible.'

At Eastnor Castle in Herefordshire, the woodland, indeed the estate as a whole, has been the principal off-road driving centre for the Land-Rover company for more than thirty years. This was another chance suggestion that has grown into a highly successful venture for both parties. James Hervey-Bathurst, whose family home this is, explains that it was his father's keen interest in agricultural engineering, and his particular love of Land-Rovers, which brought this about.

'A friend of ours recommended to the engineers at Land-Rover that they should come and drive on the estate,' he explains, 'because they were looking for somewhere to test them – somewhere steep and wet. So it started with the engineers … my father was very generous and let them drive pretty much where they wanted. They got a warm welcome and freedom to drive in the woods, on all the muddy tracks and up all the very steep hills on the edge of the Malverns. They got to like it and he was an incredibly good host, who really looked after them and was interested in what they were doing.

'Gradually more people came with them. They had foreign generals who came here to see Land-Rovers demonstrated before they signed contracts. We had a board meeting here with Michael Edwards when it was decided that Land-Rover should be set up separately from the rest of British Leyland …

'We formalised the contract in 1987. Now they have a permanent office and base here where they offer off-road driving tuition for their own employees and salesmen – and the people who buy Land-Rovers have the chance to come and practise driving them … It's a good arrangement; a happy one. They like being here and we like having them.' There's a further benefit for all concerned, in that the Land-Rover base at Eastnor provides employment, several of the people working there coming from the immediate vicinity.

While James Hervey-Bathurst oversees all aspects of the Eastnor estate, the day-to-day running of the Castle and deer park is the responsibility of his general manager, Simon Foster, who has been developing Eastnor with a definite objective in mind.

'We've got a fantastic 5,000-acre estate,' he enthuses, 'great for clay-pigeon shooting, falconry, archery, quad-biking, go-karting and all sorts of things. We've really pushed that very, very heavily. Now that Land-Rover have this major presence on the estate, we can really tap into that and offer that facility to our clients as well. So, in the corporate market, Eastnor is best known as a team-building venue and the number of days has grown very well.'

However, he adds a word of professional caution. 'I think any historic house will tell you that the corporate market generally is the most difficult one to crack.'

For many years the deer park at Eastnor has been open to caravanners. At present there are no official pitches, though licensing regulations may alter that in the near future. 'People just come in and park and it's a huge area,' Simon adds, '300 acres. On a busy bank holiday weekend we can have three or four hundred caravans.'

In addition to the touring caravans, the deer park is the setting for caravan rallies that take place throughout the year. 'There are a number of big events,' Simon continues. 'We have a big Land-Rover World event, which is a huge Land-Rover enthusiasts' event in June. We have the world's biggest twenty-four-hour mountain bike endurance event the weekend after that, called

Mountain Mayhem. We have a model and hobby show. And then the biggest event of the lot, in August, is the Big Chill, which is a pop festival for about 30,000 people.'

This is certainly a big operation, taking five weeks to set up everything needed for the three-day event and then clear everything away afterwards.

Looking ahead, Simon Foster sees the deer park as 'our really big potential growth area … There is plenty of scope to bring three or four more big events into the park during the summer. It's a question of getting them, and they're not easy to find … We are actively marketing the facility to concert promoters and event organisers. We go to exhibitions in London where we have a trade stand to try and sell Eastnor.'

However, the market is highly competitive and with a large concert featuring a well-known band costing in the region of £1,500,000 to put on, you need a lot of people attending to see a reasonable return – and Eastnor, like many historic houses, has scope to accommodate 20,000 to 30,000 people without any difficulty, as the Big Chill proves.

Each summer Powderham Castle in Devon holds a range of popular concerts. 'We have a lovely one at the end of July, which has gone on over the years, with the Bournemouth Symphony Orchestra and the Last Night of the Proms,' says Lady Devon. 'Everyone comes in through the gate from Powderham village. They park their cars and bring their picnics. We all sit looking at the stage or the Castle, which is floodlit in coloured lights. Then at the end there is a marvellous firework display synchronised with the music. That's really fun – a lovely one.

'We've also got a huge open flat space beyond [in the deer park] going down towards the estuary, where we've had bigger concerts … We got started quite early in the outdoor concert market … They were hugely popular to start with. We've had lots of big names: Shirley Bassey and Tom Jones.'

Location is important for a successful concert and Powderham is fortunate in being easily accessed from the M5, just as Eastnor is from the M50. However, the market is fairly crowded, with something like 260 outdoor concerts being held

through the UK in 2006. So promoters are having to make finely-judged decisions; for it is the promoter who bears the financial risk.

The majority of historic houses where concerts are staged solely provide the venue, leaving the installation and infrastructure for artists and audiences to the professionals, who have the equipment and experience these huge undertakings require. For large concerts, the level of organisation can be awesome. At the height of their fame, Oasis appeared at two back-to-back concerts at Knebworth. The concerts were sell-outs and with 125,000 people descending on the house and grounds for each one, nothing could be left to chance – not even the grim possibility that at least one concert-goer might never be returning home. To cover this a field mortuary was installed and happily never put to use; but, with the numbers attending, there was an actuarial possibility that it might be needed, which couldn't be overlooked.

Arrangements of this kind, catering for tens of thousands of people, would have been completely incomprehensible to the majority of historic house owners in past centuries, many of whom enjoyed the luxury of decorating and enriching their gardens and parklands according to their personal whim.

Tong Castle in Shropshire, demolished over fifty years ago, received a personal 'makeover' from one of its former owners in the early nineteenth century. George Durant II inherited his father's estate, and the fortune he made in Havana, in 1797 when he was just twenty-one. The Moorish-Gothic mansion appealed to the young man's taste, but the gardens, designed with the help of 'Capability' Brown, certainly did not match the new squire's personality.

George was rather taken with pyramids and so he had two erected, each ten feet high, on ten-feet-high gateposts either side of the main drive. Not content with that, he had an ornamental pigsty built in the shape of a pyramid, and several years later treated his chickens to a similar edifice – although this one was inscribed with various entreaties such as 'Scratch Before You Eat'.

The famous willow tree fountain at Chatsworth might well have been the inspiration for Durant to have a similar 'tree' installed at Tong Castle. Made of iron, with water pipes secreted in the trunk and branches, any unsuspecting visitor who took rest on the seat beneath the 'tree' could be immediately drenched.

In the fashion of the day George built a hermitage and while the first inhabitant lasted seven years in the employ of the Durants, his successor did not make it past four weeks. By their very nature hermits were required to live in solitary confinement, which this second occupant found too hard to bear. George's spiritual quest extended to building a pulpit by the gatehouse so that he could preach to passers-by, and to ward off anyone tempted to poach on the estate he put up a large archway made of whales' jawbones. He also had iron harps hung in various trees around the estate so that when the wind blew the harps would wail disturbingly – supposedly as a further deterrent to trespassers.

Idiosyncratic structures were not restricted to eighteenth-century flights of aristocratic fancy. In the 1930s Gerald Tyrwhitt Wilson, the 14th Baron Berners, indulged his eccentric tastes to the utmost at his home, Faringdon Park in Oxfordshire. On the front door a framed notice advised 'It is requested that all hats be removed', an elaborate chandelier hung *outside* the house, one of the bedrooms boasted a glass four-poster, and having read that in China doves were dyed with food colouring, Lord Berners decided to do the same. Consequently the Faringdon flock fluttered in all the colours of the rainbow.

In 1935 the generous baron commissioned the last major folly to be built in England. The site was already known as Folly Hill and so Lord Berners decided to put up a tower, which would give some meaning to the name. 'The great point of this tower', he said 'is that it will be entirely useless'. The architect, however, had not fully understood the brief and Lord Berners was dismayed to discover on his return from holiday that his tower was more modest and classical than he had hoped for. He insisted on adding mock battlements and various Gothic flourishes and for good measure had a sign added that read:

'Members of the public committing suicide from this tower do so at their own risk'.

While the folly on Folly Hill and the interior of Faringdon House reflected the tastes and quirks of their master, the garden was the domain of the equally eccentric Robert Heber-Percy, Lord Berners' life-long companion. There were the manicured lawns one would expect of a stately home but the row of stately urns that bordered the gravel sweep at the front of the house were filled with plastic greenery rather than the real thing; a statue of one of Britain's military legends, General Havelock, was half submerged in the lily pond because Heber-Percy thought there was nowhere else to put it; the changing room floor of the crenellated swimming pool was inlaid with thousands of pennies and the pool itself was guarded by two enormous stone wyverns.

Personal touches continue to add appeal to the gardens and grounds of historic houses today, if in rather less flamboyant ways. Mrs Clare Macpherson-Grant Russell, Laird of Ballindalloch, has six dogs, who enjoy the run of the Castle –

and tear around the grounds when the family have them to themselves. In order to make a visit to Ballindalloch Castle as enjoyable for man's best friend as it is for his or her owner, the lady Laird has provided designated shady areas where visiting dogs can be walked and left safely in cars for short periods. Fresh water is readily available for thirsty dogs to drink and for those who fancy a wash and brush-up before setting off for home, there's even a section of the Castle duck pond set aside for a refreshing four-footed dip.

'The Pearl of the North', Ballindalloch has also been called 'The castle everyone would love to live in' and that is as true for dogs as it is for their owners, since the Castle is also recognised as the most dog-friendly in the country. To confirm this, Mrs Macpherson-Grant Russell's mouth-watering recipe book, *I Love Food*, concludes with a selection of recipes for dogs: Doggie Chocolate Crunch, The Honey Bone and The Cheesey Bone.

It's certainly a castle where every keen golfer would love to live, as the Laird's husband, Oliver Russell cheerfully admits. His wife is a self-

confessed 'dogaholic' – 'The Queen has eighteen, so I have another twelve to go,' she explains.

'I'm on weak ground,' Mr Russell quickly points out, 'because my little indulgence is the golf course. Therefore I need a certain amount of operating scale to balance against that.'

The course, which lies on a gentle hillside on the banks of the River Avon that flows through the estate and joins the Spey, was actually created at the suggestion of his wife. Her husband loved golf, she reasoned, and a golf course on the estate would be a perfect addition to the sporting facilities – complementing the traditional Highland activities of fishing, shooting and stalking that attract visiting parties throughout the season. The world-renowned golf course architects Donald Steel and Tom Mackenzie were invited to design the course and they produced a par seventy-two, nine-hole course with eighteen tees. Open to all golfers, it is fully equipped with a clubhouse and affiliated PGA professional and, to quote Michael Parkinson, who clearly enjoyed his time there, 'Ballindalloch Castle Golf

Course is the perfect place to find escape from an imperfect world.'

Historic houses also provide the perfect place to escape from the modern world and catch a glimpse of life in times gone by. During the English Civil War Powderham Castle held out as a Royalist stronghold for three years, coming under siege twice from Parliamentary forces holding the nearby city of Exeter until the Castle was finally overrun in January 1646. So this makes it a popular location for battle re-enactments staged by groups like the Sealed Knot. Living in period encampments in the deer park, combatants and camp followers bring the turbulent years of the mid-seventeenth century to life, even if they do look somewhat out of place queuing outside the Powderham fish and chip shop in period costume.

Move 250 years further back to the late fourteenth century, a period evoked in Geoffrey Chaucer's *Canterbury Tales*, and falconry would have been a popular pastime for Lord Devon's ancestors, as it was for aristocrats everywhere. Although the pursuit of game birds at Powderham is now the responsibility of the three estate gamekeepers and the parties of guns they look after, the ancient falconer's skills still have a part to play in the life of the Castle. Throughout August demonstrations of a variety of birds of prey are held on the newly created North Lawn. Audience participation features prominently and allows visitors the chance to experience the same thrill of working with a trained hawk or falcon that residents and guests of Powderham Castle would have enjoyed when they hunted the estate lands beside the estuary of the River Exe centuries ago.

'There is so much to see, enjoy and appreciate that we could never take full value from it ourselves,' Lord Devon writes in his introduction to the Castle, voicing the sentiments of most historic house owners today. 'Nor, frankly, could we afford to maintain it without your help and support.'

In times gone by, falconry was a privilege reserved for his ancestors and their peers. Today, it is one of the activities included in the admission fee to Powderham Castle. The difference between 'then' and 'now' in the gardens, parks and estates of historic houses could not be more graphically illustrated.